AGITATIONS

AGITATIONS

Essays on Life and Literature

Arthur Krystal

Yale University Press   New Haven & London

Designed by James J. Johnson and set in Bulmer type by Keystone Typesetting, Inc. Printed in the United States of America.

Library of Congress Cataloging-in-Publication Data

Krystal, Arthur.

   Agitations: Essays on life and literature / Arthur Krystal.

     p. cm.

   ISBN 0-300-09216-4 (alk. paper)

   1. Books and reading. 2. Literature and society. 3. Learning and scholarship. 4. Civilization, Modern—20th century—Philosophy. I. Title.

Z1003 .K93 2002

028′.9—dc21   2002016753

A catalogue record for this book is available from the British Library.

10   9   8   7   6   5   4   3   2   1

For Solomon Krystal

Acknowledgments

The author is grateful to the following editors, who welcomed essays which often arrived unexpectedly on their doorstep: Joseph Epstein and Anne Fadiman at *The American Scholar;* Mitchel Levitas at *The New York Times Book Review,* and Lewis Lapham at *Harper's Magazine.*

Contents

What peculiar privilege has this little agitation of the brain which we call thought, that we take it to be the model of the whole universe?

DAVID HUME

Author's Note

In 1996 I published an essay in *Harper's* magazine that sought to explain my loss of interest in reading. The essay, saddled with the rather precious title of "Closing the Books: A Once-Devoted Reader Arrives at the End of the Story," created something of a stir in publishing circles and, if the letters received by *Harper's* were any indication, managed to offend readers and writers around the country. More than a few saw it as a personal affront, and one irate reader even threatened to track me down and jab me in the eye with a sharp stick. Yet the essay was not written in a spirit of contentiousness; it was meant to be provocative, of course—but not offensive. In truth, its tone was one of regret and confusion: Why should I—someone who had spent much of his life reading, editing, and writing about books—find it nearly impossible to read contemporary fiction, poetry, and criticism or, for that matter, to reread the great books of the past? The sense of loss I felt in my now severed relationship with literature was, or so I thought, the dominant motif of the essay; and while I didn't expect to receive flowers or notes of condolence, I was equally unprepared for the condemnation and anger that came my way.

Although it is nice to report that perfect strangers wrote or called to inform me that they had gone to the trouble of making copies and sending the article around to friends, I have to accept that most readers—even those not intent on punishing me—felt that I had overstated the case and was being perverse. It was, of course, just this opposition to the article that gave it a longer shelf life than it might otherwise have had. (It's not in the usual course of events that an essay on reading prompts calls from newspapers or gets its author on national radio.) And if I was surprised, it was because the essay was essentially a lament and not a condemnation of the general literary culture, and because a statement of disaffection with books is, frankly, something of a cliché.

Let me, then, say it again: Each generation is crankier than the one before and finds fault with the age and with those not as aged as oneself. Samuel Johnson, in 1753, was already fed up with people "of all degrees of ability, of every kind of education, of every profession and employment . . . posting with ardour so general to the press." Not long into the next century, Goethe pronounced himself unhappy with all the "criticizing and fragmenting journals [that] allow nothing healthy to arise"; and forty years later Thomas Carlyle noted in the *Edinburgh Review,* one of the first periodicals devoted to the reviewing of books, that "all Literature has become one boundless self-devouring Review." To those who say the times have never been so bad, I direct them to Randall Jarrell: "[Literary criticism] is not only bad or mediocre, it is *dull;* it is, often, an astonishingly graceless, joyless, humorless, long-winded, niggling, blinkered, methodical, self-important, cliché-ridden, prestige-obsessed, almost-autonomous criticism." And this was written fifty years ago.

So why did I go public with a complaint that is, after all, hardly original? For that I do have an answer. Although the complaint is a familiar one, the situation that summons it is always peculiar to one's time and place. Furthermore, whatever the respective differences in the literary world as encountered by Dr. Johnson, Goethe, Carlyle, and Jarrell, these differences did not constitute as radical a shift in the way that the generations on either side of the media and computer revolutions now experience books. Not since the invention of the printing press and the incorporation of the vernacular has literature undergone such a profound transformation. Once *the* medium to disseminate both stories and information on a wide scale, the written word now acts as a secondary method of communication. Indeed, the invasive nature of modern communications makes it difficult to retain an innocence of the world that literature once depended upon for its power.

Narratives—whatever their degree of sophistication—were, at the beginning of one's literary apprenticeship, first and foremost stories; more to the point, they were *adventure* stories—and not just novels by Zane Gray or Alexandre Dumas, but those by Charles Dickens, Henry James, and James Joyce. Because earlier generations of readers were innocent of the greater world, and because images of that world were not yet branded on their emotional retinas, even an ordinary tale or poem had an intensity about it that may no longer obtain. How many boys now read the adventures of King Arthur, Sherlock Holmes, or Tarzan with the avidity that other boys play computer games or watch movies?

These are commonplace observations. Yet for those of us who straddle the time before and after the electronic media and the computer took over the tasks of storing and conveying knowledge, the experience of reading plays out in a strange, fluctuating intellectual space. Most of us no longer read the way our parents did, and our children no longer read the way we once did. The historical particularity of reading, once conditioned by expectations of silence, privacy, solitude, as well as veneration for the book as artifact, no longer prevails. The time when children grew up exclusively listening to, or reading, stories is over: our children's epics don't take place in their heads, but rather above their heads: on a white screen in a dark theater, or at eye level on a smaller screen in their homes. Disheartening as it may be for some of us to admit, *Star Wars* and *Star Trek* are to children born after 1970 what the epic or the great novels were for earlier generations.

Having said this, it is also possible that my retreat from books is, as Jay Gatsby enigmatically put it, just personal. An intellectual grumpiness may simply be a function of aging—that is, there may come a time in life when art reflects more than it affects temperament. Although books have lost their power to move me, I still need to be moved by them. "Closing the Books" not only expresses my sadness over the end of my affair with books; it also seeks to understand it because, oddly enough, I still think of myself as a fairly tolerant reader. It's no secret that the mind, like the joints, stiffens with age, and therefore the main line of defense against intellectual arthritis is a determined self-awareness, a willingness to concede that one dislikes something because it offends, or goes against the verities, or against one's own cherished beliefs. Reviewing the *Pisan Cantos,* the British teacher and critic C. M. Bowra threw up his hands at "the unceasing rattle, the chaotic flow, the pointless gossip, the feeble generalizations, the 'knowing' air," and so on. I'd like to think that if a work like the *Cantos* came across my desk, I'd be capable of seeing merit in it, though not everything Bowra says is wrong.

But as I look back on the literary work I produced for newspapers and journals over the past fifteen years, I see a pattern emerging that tends to contradict my own protestations of tolerance. Whereas I once wrote about books with an implicit belief in their larger purpose, I gradually came to wonder if novels and poetry in the latter part of the twentieth century can really affect how we live. I don't deny that some books enter the blood, and I think I know as well as anyone that we can form attachments to books that have deeply affected us. But the question remains: Can books be a part of our lives in the sense that they equip us better to meet the travails and accidents that we meet outside books? Literature may teach; it may give pleasure; it may console—no small accomplishments—but in the final analysis can Proust's depiction of love, or George Eliot's reflections on ambition, really influence our own actions or reactions to what life throws our way?

I am not sure of the answer, or whether there even is an answer. I do know, however, that reading is no longer a going concern in the lives of many people. But I also know that we are shaped by what happens, and to students of literature, books are a large part of what happens. So while it is possible, though exceedingly difficult, to imagine literature without Chaucer, Shakespeare, Keats, Byron, Baudelaire, Dostoevsky, Proust, Kafka, and Yeats, it is inconceivable for people who care about literature to imagine *themselves* without these authors. I may no longer read much these days, but what I once read is what compels me to write; and because of the way I used to read and the absolute faith I had in literature, I know that reading, by its very nature, remains a private act in which self-communion folds into self-realization. This doesn't contradict the usefulness of public forums, or the need for restless and divergent critical approaches—but because all too often these days the wrong people seem to teach or write about books, it is all the more gratifying when a maverick professor such as Harold Bloom directs us to a simple truth: "You cannot teach someone to love great poetry if they come to you without such love. How can you teach solitude?"

1

Closing the Books:
A Devoted Reader Arrives at the End of the Story

———

Several years ago, a man I knew, an assistant professor of English at an Ivy League university, decided to scrap his library—a gesture that at the time did not properly impress me. What interested me were the books themselves, as I was one of those invited to plunder the novels, biographies, anthologies of plays and poetry, works of criticism, short-story collections, a sampling of history and philosophy—exactly what you'd expect from a lifetime of liberal-arts collecting. The reason he gave them away, and the reason I didn't catch on to what was really happening, is that he had been offered a job in Hollywood. The money was the usual ridiculous amount by any standard but Hollywood's, and the man had a family to support. I figured that he was merely switching careers and the books were extra weight, intellectual baggage he wouldn't need out there.

Still, I should have realized that something else was going on. Leaving academia doesn't require leaving one's books behind, nor does quitting teaching necessarily suppose a disaffection with literature. Indeed, given what English departments are like these days, it may actually attest to a love of books. And though the professor in question wasn't happy with the direction that literature studies were taking in the Seventies and Eighties, this was not the reason he gave up teaching. Other professors of English find the current theoretical and political atmosphere disagreeable without running off to the hills, Beverly or otherwise. They stick it out because literature, despite what many of their colleagues profess, remains for them the artistic form in which an individual's awareness of life encounters its fullest expression.

So it wasn't just dissatisfaction with the academic scene that prompted this man to empty his bookshelves. Despite his professional gripes, he was looking forward to a successful career. He was not much past thirty, he already had one book to his credit, and was contributing articles and book reviews to leading newspapers and magazines. This is no small point. His work was showing up in places where most English teachers would give their eyeteeth to appear. But he chose to give it up; he chose Hollywood over both the academic and the literary life, and the point I had missed was not that he was switching careers but that he was switching identities. He had stopped living for literature, and literature in turn would no longer provide him with a living.

At the time, such a feeling—or rather loss of feeling—for books was unthinkable to me. After years of bumming around and working at a variety of blue-collar jobs, I had begun to do some editing and writing myself, and though I was never in the thick of things—being part of neither the neoconservative crowd at *Commentary* and the *New Criterion* nor the liberal crowd at the *Village Voice* and the *New York Times*—I kept up with developments in the academy and publishing alike. Gradually I, too, began reviewing for half a dozen newspapers and journals, and bookshelves had to be built to accommodate the titles that came my way. I didn't keep every book that landed on my desk, and every so often I would weed out the unwanted or unread, but the idea of seeing my books scattered on the floor or dumped unceremoniously in boxes for others to cart off was unimaginable. Now, however, in my mid-forties the idea is not so ridiculous. For some reason or conflation of reasons, I no longer care so much for literature, and certainly even less for the literary life.

This may not strike many people as a statement fraught with drama, but for someone who grew up in a bookish household, whose first friends were those he could discuss books with, and for whom the writing and teaching of books always seemed an inevitability, a loss of interest in literature is no less a palpable sensation than falling out of love. To be and then not to be in love is to undergo some radical change in personality. Not only do we experience the loss of connection to another but something is also missing in one's relation to oneself. In some way, the person one used to be is now gone.

What I used to be is "literary," by which I mean something both specific and at the same time indefinable. Superficially, it betokens a familiarity with the usual suspects among Dead White Males (and a few Females), a familiarity that makes it possible to recognize a poet or novelist by virtue of his or her music, syntax, rhetorical flourishes, or subject matter. At the very least, it means being able to situate a poem or prose work within a fifty-year period. When I was in college, friends would choose a book at random, keeping the cover hidden, and begin to read from the middle, omitting only proper names. The trick was to identify the author. Those of us who grew up reading the Great (and not-so-great) Books usually managed to guess correctly. We recognized the music without knowing the name of the composition because we took for granted a writer's singularity; distinguishing between John Keats and John Clare was as natural as distinguishing between types of flora, and those incapable of noting differences in technique and level of skill eventually dropped away.

Surely some act of nature is at work here, a predisposition similar to perfect pitch and the ability to think musically. But if being literary is an accident of birth, it is also subject to life's accidents, which can either thwart or stimulate it, and this is where a definition of "literary" becomes tricky. It's easy enough to say that books are important, but what exactly does this mean? Just how *necessary* are Proust, Henry James, Joyce, Dante, Baudelaire, Wordsworth? Has reading them truly affected the course of my life in anything but a professional sense? Although a book may sometimes overwhelm the idealistic or easily impressionable (*The Sorrows of Young Werther* led to a spate of suicides after its publication in 1774), does literature—with the exception of the Bible—really affect our dealings with others?

There was a time not so long ago when books were essential in a way that now seems almost mythical, when the bond between life and literature was a fact that brooked no dispute among men and women of letters. People may not have read as if their lives depended on it (as the poet Adrienne Rich would have us believe she did), but books did matter for Mark Pattison, Matthew Arnold, Virginia Woolf, and Lionel Trilling in a way that is alien to most contemporary readers. Fifty years ago a different set of expectations were in place: "It was as if we didn't know where we ended and books began," Anatole Broyard recalled of his life in Greenwich Village. "Books were our weather, our environment, our clothing. We didn't simply read books; we became them. We took them into ourselves and made them into our histories. . . . Books gave us balance. . . . Books steadied us. . . . They gave us gravity."

What literary person has not felt the same? Like Broyard, I grew up inside books. In my parents' home and in the homes of my childhood friends, the European masters—Goethe, Schiller, Balzac, Dostoevsky, Tolstoy—were revered as commentators on the social and human condition (the two being, in fact, one). I read as a matter of course; it was nothing to read six novels a week when I was fourteen; I probably thought everyone did. And I continued reading at this clip even while in college, or traveling, or hanging ceilings at the Charleston Navy yards.

It was only when I began reviewing books on a regular basis in the early 1980s that I found I had to cut back. Note-taking, thinking, and writing take time. Still, I read more than I was paid to read, if only because a reviewer's responsibility extends beyond the book at hand. And as happens to all novice reviewers, the glow soon faded from seeing my name in print. But something unexpected also happened: my desire to read faded as well—almost to the vanishing point.

These days, the newspaper, two or three magazines, and the occasional thriller are all that I can manage. Recently, I tried re-reading Henry James's *The Ambassadors,* a novel that I admired when I was in graduate school, but put it aside after three pages. It was as if I'd forgotten how to swim, or, if not quite that, as if reading it wasn't worth the effort. Nor does it seem worth the effort to peruse the various book-review sections, literary journals, or publishers' catalogues, all of which at one time were pabulum to me. Even bookstores are not the magnets they used to be, not even secondhand ones, which for any real lover of books are what the sirens were to Odysseus. As for reviewing, the idea of writing about another contemporary novel or work of criticism has about as much appeal as spending a night in a bus station. In short, I am out of it: I don't give a damn who or what gets published these days, and I can't imagine why anyone would.

In case someone might think that I suffer from reviewer's fatigue, let me quash the notion. I was the occasional reviewer, averaging twelve or fifteen reviews a year. I couldn't hold a candle to someone like George Orwell, who reviewed eight or ten books a month for months at a time, and for whom "the prolonged, indiscriminate reviewing of books [was] a quite exceptionally thankless, irritating and exhausting job." If it were only reviewing that had

caused me to stop reading books, I wouldn't be terribly concerned. A little rest and recreation, and I'd be set to read again. But
the disinclination goes deeper. Something is wrong that has nothing to do with reading and writing on assignment. It's difficult to
say why, or even to be sure that I have given up on books perma-
nently, but the fact that I can contemplate a life without literature
is, to put it mildly, bizarre.

Do I have to add that this is not how literary people are
supposed to feel? The only writer I know of who professed to be
bored by books was Philip Larkin: "Don't read much now: the
dude / Who lets the girl down before / The hero arrives, the chap /
Who's yellow and keeps the store, / Seem far too familiar. Get
stewed: / Books are a load of crap." It's hard to know how serious
Larkin was—he seems to be speaking mainly of adventure stories
here—but there is something to what he says. After thirty or forty
years of reading in a serious way, a person may be excused for
finding many newly minted novels and poems far too familiar.
"The flesh is sad, alas! and I have read all the books," Mallarmé
observed. He hadn't, of course, but we know what he means.

A long time ago I used to read for the sheer pleasure of it.
Words on a page, whether written by Edgar Rice Burroughs or
Ford Madox Ford—to name two writers who are probably not
smoking a cigar together in the afterlife—absorbed me. It didn't
matter that one was a "serious" writer and the other a "hack";
both managed to keep me interested. I knew without having to be
taught (writers themselves were sufficient to teach me) which
works were profound, shallow, mannered, innovative, raw, or
cooked. A good teacher or critic was often valuable in pointing out
textual subtleties or providing an historical gloss, but to be honest
I can't recall any professor significantly altering my view of a poet's
or novelist's merits. And I still like the writers I used to like; it's just
that I don't plan to renew my acquaintance with them.

When I mention my disaffection to friends, they invariably attribute it to the literary climate. "Of course you're depressed. Who isn't these days?" But that explanation doesn't really work for me. After all, people have always complained about bad books and stupid reviews. Self-promoters, blurbmeisters, and hucksters are as old as the troubadours. "[I]t is scarcely possible nowadays to tell the reviews from the advertising," groused Edmund Wilson. "[B]oth tend to convey the impression that masterpieces are being manufactured as regularly as new models of motorcars." The year is 1926 and Wilson goes on to say, "The present writers on American literature all have interests in one phase or another of it: either the authors know one another personally or they owe one another debts of gratitude or they are bound together by their loyalty to some stimulating common cause. And almost all forget critical standards in their devotion to the great common causes."

Wilson himself, incidentally, was not above promoting writers whom he liked or had slept with, and only the terminally naive could think that things have changed much. So if I can't blame the insularity of the book business for what ails me, what can I blame? Well, the academy comes to mind, that confederation of professors and curricula which over the last three decades has reversed the respective status of criticism and belles lettres, and in the process managed to drive a wedge between the intellectual and the literary life.

As recently as thirty years ago, to be literary was by definition to be intellectual. Intellectuals, whether or not inclined to produce poems or novels, were duty-bound to evaluate them, and these evaluations when undertaken by the likes of Matthew Arnold, T. S. Eliot, Randall Jarrell, R. P. Blackmur, and M. H. Abrams often approached something like literature itself. But with the advent of the deconstructionist/semiotic/historicist/gender-based criticism that gained currency during the 1970s, men of letters such as Saint-Beuve and Lionel Trilling were relegated to the back of the intellectual bus, while the theorists—Barthes, Benjamin, Derrida, Adorno, de Man, Foucault, Lacan, Bakhtin—sat up front. Actually they drove the bus, and the attention lavished on them altered the course of literary studies, making it retrograde to uphold the aesthetic qualities that once distinguished literature from other forms of written discourse.

As someone who felt that the great writers, despite their personal failings, had more to teach us than those who taught by diminishing their works, I did not take kindly to the exaltation of theory. Nor did I care for the fact that my own essays and book reviews were being held accountable to some putatively democratic ideal that discouraged harsh appraisals of well-intentioned books. One book review editor, for example, was unhappy with my misgivings about the politically correct orthodoxy demonstrated by *The Columbia History of the American Novel.* My objections to the way literature was being taught were taken as a political statement by a newspaper that did not want to be seen as condoning such unfashionable views. The irony is (and it can be ironic only in this climate) that my politics, such as they are, are anything but conservative. Endorsing the canon does not mean that I vote the Republican ticket.

Edmund Wilson didn't know how good he had it. But bad as things are today, I can't really blame my reading problem on the depredations of either the writers or the professors. Although I am convinced that no writer of the past generation has improved upon Nabokov, Borges, Wallace Stevens, Dylan Thomas, Philip Larkin, and W. H. Auden, someone else has every right to feel differently. My own unshakable conviction is that contemporary novels and poems are ordinary, not because of their subject matter (which may be sensational) but because our expectations of literature are so ordinary. We don't expect greatness of our writers, and perhaps we don't want it. We are satisfied with Jay McInerney, E. L. Doctorow, Anne Tyler, David Leavitt, and Joyce Carol Oates. Just so there is no confusion, I'm perfectly happy to admit that Richard

Ford, Cormac McCarthy, Richard Russo, Cynthia Ozick, and a dozen other novelists are worth reading; it's just that I don't see why I should read them.

As for contemporary poetry, the secret is out. Some of the poetry of the last quarter century isn't bad, and some of Elizabeth Bishop's and Richard Wilbur's is quite good, but the vast majority has neither beauty nor passion nor the power to move us. Is it just my imagination or do critics of poetry overcompensate, assigning greatness where there is only intelligence and competence? Read, say, Helen Vendler on practically anyone and you will be impressed by her insights and references; then read the poetry itself and you have to wonder what inspired her acts of exegetical devotion.

Most readers, however, are afraid to question the experts—afraid of appearing too dense to appreciate a poem by James Merrill or Jorie Graham, afraid of being taken for the sort of person who looks at an expressionist painting and says, "My ten-year-old kid could do that." I don't know what's worse: the philistine who will not make the attempt to grasp the unfamiliar, or the half-smart, half-literary reader who, because the *New Yorker* or the *New York Review of Books* runs high-sounding critical essays, thinks that John Ashbery and Rita Dove are poets of the first rank.

Because plenty of other readers feel the same way and haven't given up on reading, I don't see how I can connect my loss of interest in books to the dearth of great writers today. Moreover, I still believe that Homer, Dante, Shakespeare, Keats, and Joyce deflate every theorist, multiculturalist, or product of a creative writing workshop now forcing his attentions on us. At the same time, however, I feel little desire to reread the Great Books. And that is what's baffling, because it was not supposed to turn out this way. When I was young it was axiomatic that a deeper appreciation of books came with age. I remember my parents telling me that Dostoevsky could not really be understood until one was forty, a

figure that was amended upward as they got older. And Henry
James was always spoken of as someone who improves with age,
the reader's age, that is. I've never doubted this—at least not
until now.

Let me see if I can explain it. Once we have come to appreciate
the difficulty of writing, once we have been duly impressed by the
poet's or the novelist's genius, once we have read the salient criticism, we are left alone with our thoughts—thoughts unlike those
we had when books themselves were tantamount to experiences,
part of what formed us. At fifteen or twenty, the books we read—or
rather the minds behind them—are far more interesting than our
own. But as we experience for ourselves the rites of passage that
were previously only read about, and as we mature and reflect on
what those experiences mean, novelists and poets begin to lose an
important advantage—at some point we've all been down the same
road. And what may happen is this: we begin to find that most
writers are less interesting than we think ourselves to be.

I don't know if much has been written about the relationship
between aging and reading, but it seems to me, given my own long-
standing investment in books, that a rather increasingly fine equation does exist. How one reads at twenty and forty (and sixty, I
expect) are experiences both subtly and conspicuously different. I
attach no profundity to this observation. I merely point out that
the relationship is not often talked about. Call it the biology of
taste, for if I'm right, there may be a connection between hormonal
balance and the patience required to read serious fiction and poetry. In my own case, the difference between my reading habits
today and twenty years ago is about as dramatic as the change in
my eyesight. Nowadays I require what are called reading glasses,
an irony too obvious to dwell on.

At one time, books, especially novels, could actually change
the way I felt about the world. Yet this capacity to be amazed and
shaped by books has, in my case at least, proved to be temporal.

Books that managed to fuel my imagination at fifteen or twenty-five now seem overwrought, self-indulgent, or simply irrelevant. Nor is it only the eccentric or peripheral poet or playwright—Lautréamont, Nerval, Roussell, Jarré—who has lost his hold on me, but also those writers who deal with the human condition in all its breadth and complexity. It's easy enough to understand how one might put aside Villiers de L'Isle-Adam ("As for living, our servants will do that for us"), but how do I come to terms with casting out Tolstoy and George Eliot?

The sad truth is, I am unable to think seriously about any writer. Instead I think about what every middle-aged, nonliterary person thinks about: family, health, health insurance, money, property, time running out, and so on. Why this should interfere with or diminish one's capacity to appreciate literature is not hard to understand. But, by the same token, there are people who turn to literature to understand the mundane, who find in poetry and fiction not so much an escape as an avenue to thoughts so beautifully or interestingly expressed that they may be tested against reality. Indeed, one could argue that life itself sharpens our appreciation of novels, allowing us to see how a writer handles the particularities of experience, how he or she makes the familiar seem new and even transcendent.

Conceding this, I still maintain there comes a point when one "outgrows" novels, at least in the sense that the words no longer speak to one's experience in a way that reveals new depth about that experience. Matters of technique and felicitous phrasing aside, contemporary novels about marital relationships, friendship, parenting, mental illness, homosexuality, or coming of age do not persuade me that anything new is being added to the store of literature. Here is the crux, absurdly simple: once you have made the acquaintance of truly interesting minds, minds such as Montaigne's, Shakespeare's, Goethe's, Swift's, Diderot's, Nietzsche's, Mallarmé's, Dostoevsky's, Wilde's—even if you disagree with some of their ideas, and even if you detect signs of ingrained cultural bias—what do the novels and poems of today have to offer other than implicit commentary on their antecedents? Another way of saying this is: the best is the enemy of the good, and once you have become acquainted with the former, why bother with the rest?

What happened? What happened to the capacity to feel the possibilities in books? To answer this, I have to summon up the way books used to make me feel, and when I consider the eagerness with which I set out to read everything I could, and how a peculiar book like Djuna Barnes's *Nightwood* once made me whistle in amazement, it seems to me that a necessary component of the literary life is a certain romantic attachment to life itself. But life is not very romantic these days. I'm not sure it ever was, but at least in the days before the media transformed the nature of existence by devaluing the idea of privacy, a writer's imaginative powers and a reader's imaginative responses were shaped by a real sense of possibility. The greater world, being further removed from the ordinary individual, required an imaginative leap to bring it home. And when the imagination succeeded through print or pigment, one felt the jolt, the power of art to transfigure one's life.

Now it is our expectations that have been transformed. What previously was regarded as profane (and therefore also sacred, in terms of being removed from ordinary discourse and experience) is now insistently made public; we expect as a matter of course to witness communally what formerly we read about alone. The things we do in private seem merely prelude to what is revealed in public. Nowadays, Anna Karenina doesn't head for the railroad tracks; instead, she and Vronsky take their sad tale to Phil Donahue or some other talk show host. And after Heathcliff and

Cathy fight it out in the tabloids, they reconcile and make for the nearest downtown club.

Because on some basic level we read to spy on other people—whether they lie in bed all day like Oblomov or hop into bed with others like Emma Bovary—why should we bother to open a book when we can witness fear and loathing on the TV screen: actual people screaming, sobbing, accusing or forgiving their spouses, lovers, parents, or children in the privacy of our own homes? A "privacy" unlike that of other ages, when solitude meant being unable to see *out* as well as others being unable to see in. The reason novels are no longer news is not simply that the news can now be electronically transmitted but that the integrity of once private and powerful emotions has been cheapened by the nature and volume of our public discourse. How can novels thrive in an environment that prides itself on the outpouring of naked emotion?

One also has to wonder whether the public display of what are essentially moral concerns does not, in effect, debase the very idea of morality. When matters fit for private contemplation or family discussion are thrust in our faces, we lose sight of the fact that morality is ultimately an individual concern, not a sideshow disguised as a public forum. This is where the novelist once held sway, in the depiction of the individual's struggle with familial and societal values and the resulting emotional turmoil when conventional morality was flouted. To a large extent, the great novels of the past were morality plays spun into art through characters whose souls and minds wrestled with concepts such as "sin," "duty," "pride," "propriety," "virtue," "ambition," and "honor." These words were not used to entertain, and they were not fodder for morning talk shows; they were the stuff of conscience, with enough resonance to power a plot for three hundred pages. No more. Morality is no longer part of the novelist's stock-in-trade—it seems more the province of PC militants, evangelists, and right-wing bigots—and when manners and morals lose relevance for the greater community, the power of novels to move us is similarly diminished.

None of which deters our poets and novelists from their self-appointed rounds. The literary world perpetuates itself like any solid enterprise that depends on product perception. Writers write, reviewers review, publishers publish, and new books come down the pike with pomp and circumstance (80,000 in the United Kingdom per annum; 49,000 in the United States). For those still inclined to read contemporary fiction and poetry, this is good news indeed.

As for me, newspapers, magazines, and mysteries are quite sufficient, although to be honest, I still dip into the odd poet or essayist now and then; old habits die hard and good writing (in small doses) still gives me a boost. For example, I recently came across what I consider to be a particularly brilliant, absolutely dead-on literary essay, full of sharp and relevant insights, although somewhat musty in its locution. It begins, "I hate to read new books." And goes on to say, "Books have in a great measure lost their power over me; nor can I revive the same interest in them as formerly. I perceive when a thing is good, rather than feel it. . . . If any one were to ask me what I read now, I might answer with my Lord Hamlet in the play—'Words, words, words.'"

The essay is Hazlitt's *On Reading Old Books*. It was published in 1821, which presents a problem to this writer, since what Hazlitt regarded as "the dust and smoke and noise of modern literature" pales by comparison with what's going on today. Hazlitt, however, was being a bit disingenuous, striking an ominous note to get the reader's attention, then quickly mellowing. He acknowledges re-visiting old favorites as well as having plans to examine many plays, speeches, and histories hitherto unread. About novels he is less sanguine, though he intends, he says, to look at Walter Scott's "last new novel (if I could be sure it was so)."

I'm afraid that Hazlitt was a more devout reader than I can claim to be. Nonetheless, I think it more than a coincidence that old Bill was forty-three when he wrote the above, about the same age I was when I began to hate new books. Of course, if Hazlitt had lived another hundred years and refused to read new books, the number of remarkable books denied him would be formidable. Does this mean that I'm wrong? Perhaps. But somehow I doubt it. Hazlitt lived at a time when literature—and novels in particular— circumvented the cultural limitations imposed on public and private discourse. Thoughts that could not be spoken of—between husband and wife, mother and daughter—found their voice in fictional creations. This voice persists, of course, although it now seems hopelessly muted. I don't mean simply that literature is being shouted down by the media but that poets and novelists somehow know deep in their bones that their work no longer possesses the cultural resonance that writers could once take for granted. Surely such knowledge must account in part for the rather undistinguished work that passes for literary art these days. Writers, in sum, are not to be envied: they know they cannot compete with the age, but, being writers, they also know that they cannot withdraw. Readers, on the other hand, can.

So good luck to all the poems, novels, plays, memoirs, and new translations of the *Iliad* and the *Inferno* that will get written from now to whenever. Among all these there will surely be one or two of surpassing beauty and wisdom, but I shall not—unless a friend hits me over the head with them—learn of their existence. And for the time being, this does not seem so great a sacrifice to make.

[1996]

2

H. C. Witwer and Me:
The Making of a Reader

————

H. C. Witwer's 1920 novel *The Leather Pushers* went for a song at the auction of boxing books and ephemera at New York's Swann Galleries in January 1997. One of six books in Lot 51, which included Budd Schulberg's *The Harder They Fall* and Harold Ribalow's *World's Greatest Boxing Stories,* it was not among the sale's more celebrated titles. My paddle was up at eighty dollars, again at ninety, and then I made my mistake. I began to think. Five of the books didn't matter to me, and ninety-five dollars is pretty steep for a book that isn't a collector's item. On the other hand, I had been looking for *The Leather Pushers* for fifteen years, which comes to about seven dollars a year, counting the buyer's premium. While I was considering all this, the lot was sold to a man one row in front of me for a hundred dollars.

Had I been wearing ten-ounce gloves, I would have beaten myself up. I was a piker, a cheapskate, a dope. But perhaps all was not lost. During the break I approached the newest owner of *The Leather Pushers* and wondered whether he might consider parting with it for a fair price. Naturally, he cocked his head at this. Did I know something he did not? Having satisfied himself that I was neither a collector nor a dealer, merely an eccentric, this splendid fellow, a partner in the brokerage house of McFadden, Farrel & Smith, announced that he would make a present of it. I, of course, wouldn't hear of such a thing. He, of course, would hear of nothing else. A week later Witwer's novel arrived in the mail.

An exultant moment, yet not without a vague anxiety. Suddenly I wasn't sure that I wanted to revisit a book I had left behind such a long time ago. Instead of devouring it, I was content simply to handle it, a well-preserved 1921 cloth edition of 341 pages with a cover illustration of two fighters flailing against a splattered red-and-white background. True, I could not resist glancing occasionally at the first paragraph, which to my relief was competently written; but then I'd put the book aside, as if not to push my luck. Finally, after a few nights of dithering, I took it to bed. I surged past the first paragraph, the first page, the second, and gradually it came to me: the reason that I had hunted it down long after forgetting just about everything in it.

To be honest, I had even forgotten the book's title and author. This was a novel I had last read in 1961, when I was fourteen, and aside from the hero's name—his ring name: Kid Roberts—all I could remember was that he had gone to Harvard; that his tycoon father naturally deplored his brutal vocation; that the beautiful and classy girl who loved him also deplored his brutal vocation; and that Harvard notwithstanding, the Kid goes on to become the heavyweight champion of the world. I was fourteen, what did I know?

Maybe because it had been borrowed from a classmate or maybe because the sixties had efficiently sutured off my adolescence, I forgot all about the novel. So complete was its obliteration that I actually picked up a paperback copy of *The Leather Pushers* at the auction preview without any bells going off. Only the name

"Kid Roberts" on the back cover alerted me to the fact that *this* was the book. A moment later, the cloth edition turned up.

Recovering memories is a mysterious process. Fifteen years earlier, while I was explaining to a bemused young woman my interest in boxing and boxing literature, the name Kid Roberts, without warning, without the slightest tectonic shift in memory, suddenly burst from oblivion. One moment the novel wasn't there, the next instant it was, and though the characters and plot were all muddled, I remembered distinctly how it felt to have read it. I was nuts about the book. It was what stories and reading stories was all about. And by God, I was going to find it.

I saw myself as a svelte Caspar Gutman traveling the world over in search of the black bird. But without benefit of title or author, mine was a rather messy quest. I asked around—but the people who knew literature didn't know beans about boxing books, and the people who knew boxing didn't read all that much. I checked out every secondhand bookstore in every city I visited, looking for—well, anything that might lead me further. I found plenty of rare books that way, including a copy of Conan Doyle's *The Croxley Master and Other Tales of the Ring and Camp,* but no novels about a fighter named Kid Roberts. One winter afternoon in the multi-lampshaded reading room of the New York Public Library, I ran my eye down tiny-lettered columns in old volumes of *Books in Print.* What was I looking for?

In time a search takes on a life of its own. Unless the longed-for object is of inherent value—a jewel-encrusted falcon—it becomes secondary to the search itself. *The Leather Pushers* was just a book, but it was a book I read when there had been no end to novels every bit as wonderful as those by H. C. Witwer, when practically every novel that fell into my hands seemed absolutely right. At fourteen, I read quickly, furiously, compulsively. I went through five, six novels a week or suffered from withdrawal. Reading at this pace is not unique among the bookish young, but as with any obsession, there is something faintly suspect about it, as if the allure of books is a comment on the pleasures to be found outside books.

L ove of reading, or a reading dependency, is a phenomenon often acknowledged by those incapable of stopping. In *Reading: An Essay,* one of five small books in J. B. Priestley's Pleasures of Life series, Hugh Walpole divides readers into two general categories: the ecstatic and the critical, allowing of course for the inevitable overlap. Whether one becomes one kind of reader or the other, according to Walpole, depends on "some dominating influence" that appears in the life of every future reader, usually at the age of fourteen or fifteen, "that solves, partly, the question as to whether he will be in later life an aesthetic or unaesthetic reader."

For Walpole, it was Walter Scott's Waverley novels that sent him tumbling down the ecstatic path. He became what I. A. Richards used to call "a swoon reader." Scott did it for me, too, but he had help from Rafael Sabatini, Alexandre Dumas *père,* Victor Hugo, Robert Louis Stevenson, James Fenimore Cooper, Jules Verne, Jack London, the two Edgars—Allan Poe and Rice Burroughs—and, yes, H. C. Witwer. Fourteen seems to be a magic age for the confirmed reader. In "The Lost Childhood," his short essay on becoming a writer, Graham Greene asked:

> What do we ever get nowadays from reading to equal the excitement and the revelation in those first fourteen years? Of course I should be interested to hear that a new novel by Mr. E. M. Forster was going to appear this Spring, but I could never compare that mild expectation of civilized pleasure with the missed heartbeat, the appalled glee I felt when I found on a library shelf a novel by Rider Haggard, Percy Westerman, Captain Brereton or Stanley Weyman.

When Greene was fourteen, his library shelf delivered up Marjorie Bowen's novel *The Viper of Milan* and "for better or worse the future was struck. From that moment [he] began to write." Much as I'd like to say that *The Leather Pushers* made me into a writer, or even a golden-glove novice, I'm afraid it wouldn't be true. Still, I can recall the "missed heartbeat, the appalled glee" I felt when the sequel to *The Three Musketeers* fell into my clutches. To be young was bookish heaven. At fourteen I read every word of every page; I didn't know you *could* skip words. Why should I when all authors were infallible; all narrators, reliable; every detail, essential? Digressions simply did not exist. Even the famously long dissertation on the battle of Waterloo in *Les Misérables* was enthralling, as timely and material as any other scene.

And reading was fun—not serious fun, mind you, but sequestered, magical, self-absorbed fun. Nothing mattered but the story: who won, who survived, who ended up happy, who came up short. Moreover, all novels—adventure, historical, and fantasy—were on a par; all were equally good. If someone had told me then that the books featuring Tarzan, Scaramouche, the Count of Monte Cristo, Ivanhoe, Jean Valjean, Long John Silver, and Kid Roberts had been written by a single person using seven pseudonyms, I would have concurred at once.

Not that I entirely agree with Walpole. The nature of reading is less definitive than Walpole's claims for it. Sure, there are swoon readers, but the swooning is modulated by the years. Once the young reader gets past the stage where the brain sucks in books as if they were bubbles of oxygen, he or she begins to sense that Melville is doing something different from Steinbeck, and that Dickens and Balzac resemble each other in certain respects, but not in all. As children we crossed wide-eyed and trusting into the writer's world; as adults we invite the writer into ours and hold him accountable for how he behaves there.

Walpole erred on the side of optimism, trusting too much in the ecstatic reader's resilience. Surely brevity is part of the ecstatic condition, and by omitting to put temporal brackets around ecstasy, Walpole conveniently forgot that reading evolves into the more or less critical. Schooling and swooning don't mesh, and once we begin to differentiate between the rhetorical devices that stylistically and thematically inform different narratives, the innocence, the thrill, the trusting acceptance disappear. Replaced, to be sure, by the edifying feeling that one is learning something valuable. And, of course, there is pleasure to be had from analysis, but it is a more complicated pleasure than giving oneself over completely to stories. However you slice it, reading critically is a more solemn affair than reading ecstatically.

"The books one reads in childhood, and perhaps most of all bad and good bad books," George Orwell mused, "create in one's mind a sort of false map of the world, a series of fabulous countries into which one can retreat at odd moments." At fourteen, I think I knew that boxing was not a happy or noble profession, but books about it did, in fact, become fabulous countries. From *The Leather Pushers* I went on to find Nat Fleischer's *Pictorial History of Boxing,* which steered me to W. C. Heinz's *Fireside Book of Boxing,* which drew me to biographies of John L. Sullivan and Joe Louis; and eventually I encountered the marvelous A. J. Liebling, and through Liebling, Pierce Egan, the first chronicler of the London Prize Ring.

Those repelled by boxing, or simply indifferent, may be surprised to learn of the vast literature devoted to it. R. A. Hartley's *History and Bibliography of Boxing Books* mentions 2,100 pugilistic titles published in the English language. One finds in it such names as Thackeray, Dickens, Byron, Hazlitt, Arthur Conan Doyle, Bernard Shaw, and Arnold Bennett. American authors are represented by Jack London, Nelson Algren, James T. Farrell, Heywood Broun, Hemingway, Mailer, and Joyce Carol Oates. Witwer merits nine

entries, which are immediately followed by four for P. G. Wodehouse. So many scribes of the scuffle, one ponders, so many literary
eminencies drawn to the sport.

S o who was H. C. Witwer? I didn't know. I didn't even know
what his initials stood for, since the 1921 Grosset & Dunlap
edition I now owned neglects to say. But I knew where to look.
Page 290 of volume 21 of the *National Cyclopaedia of American Biography* shows one column of seventy-five lines for Harry
Charles Witwer—not a bad testimonial for a writer no one remem-
bers. Of German extraction, Witwer was born in 1890 in Athens,
Pennsylvania, and died thirty-nine years later in Los Angeles. A
short life, but one that netted him a considerable reputation as
journalist, humorist, fiction writer, and screenwriter. As a young
man in Philadelphia, Witwer held down a bunch of odd jobs—
errand boy, hotel clerk, salesman, fight manager—before landing a
position with the *St. Cloud* (Florida) *Tribune.* From there he
moved on to the *New York American,* the *Brooklyn Eagle,* and the
New York Sun, for whom he covered World War I.

"Meantime his attempts to write conventional magazine fiction in correct English were unsuccessful," moralizes the *National
Cyclopaedia.* "Ordinary language failed him as an effective vehicle
for his vein of humor." Indeed, had it not been for Mrs. Witwer,
clearly an estimable woman and critic, *The Leather Pushers* might
never have become my pugilistic Rosebud. It was she who "finally
set him on the right path by suggesting that he write as he spoke,"
the result being an "unexampled outflow of slang stories . . . and
with the first one printed he won the interest of the large American
reading public which prefers its fiction in the vernacular." Just in
case we didn't get it the first time: "He achieved a colossal popu-
larity by producing on paper a manner of speaking rather than of
writing." During a fifteen-year period, Witwer published four hun-

dred stories, twenty-five screenplays, fourteen novels, and four plays. *Whew,* to use the vernacular.

When Mrs. Witwer advised her husband to write as he spoke, she was clearly giving the raspberry to Comte de Buffon's dictum that "those who write as they speak, even though they speak well, write badly." Knowing instinctively that such a rule applies less scrupulously if one speaks like a mook to begin with, Mrs. Witwer urged her husband on. A good thing, too. Witwer's prose is brisk, workmanlike, and certainly superior to that found in the story weeklies, dime novels, and hundreds of pulp magazines that ca-tered to the tastes of a vernacular-preferring public.

> Me and Cockeyed Egan was tourin' "God's Own Country" (Russian for the West), where the natives would rather be Harold Bell Wright than be president, each with a stable of battlers, picking up *beaucoup* sugar by havin' 'em fight each other over the short routes, when Kane Halliday skidded across my path. Besides Beansy Mullen and Bearcat Reed, a coupla heavies, I had a good welter in Battlin' Lewis, and Egan had K. O. Krouse, another tough boy, which made up a set. Them last two babies mixed with each other more times a month than a chorus girl uses a telephone.

Although Witwer wrote about the sharpies, hustlers, louts, and swaggerers of the sporting world, he wrote about them with élan. Loftiness is a question more of style than of substance. And perhaps with the good Mrs. Witwer proofing the pages as they rolled off the Underwood, H. C. mined a vein of hard-boiled prose that appealed to the audience that pshawed the pulps. He wrote with a wink and a nudge, his style an implicit compact between author and reader in which each knows better than the malaprop-isms and solecisms that bedeck the printed page. In short, we and Witwer are in cahoots. Twain had already led the way with Tom and Huck, and if Harry Witwer is not Mark Twain, neither is he

any less proficient than Damon Runyon at conjuring up an urban
America that was beginning to strut its stuff in books and movies.
The obvious resemblance, of course, is to his exact contemporary
Ringold Wilmer Lardner who, although a more serious and more
subtle comic writer, might have no cause to resent comparison.

Having now reread *The Leather Pushers,* I am amazed at how
much must have gone right by me. Who in blazes is Harold
Bell Wright and why would some people rather be him than be
president? (Wright was a best-selling novelist ninety years ago,
author of *The Winning of Barbara Worth* and *The Shepherd of the
Hills,* which romanticized the lives of country folk.) Other allu-
sions to historical figures and events—"He won more gold and
silver cups than the Crown Prince lifted from Belgium"—also
could have made no sense to a fourteen-year-old. But what did it
matter? The prose had verve, it had attitude. Here the Kid is
introduced:

> This guy had been committed to college with the idea that
> when he'd come out he'd be at the very least a civil engineer,
> though most of the engineers I know learned their trade in a
> round-house and yard and was civil enough as far as that part
> of it goes. Halliday's people was supposed to have a dollar for
> every egg in a shad roe, and the boy treated the civil engineer
> thing as a practical joke and college as somethin' he had been
> gave for Christmas to play with.

I can't say I feel a swoon coming on, but I do see how an
adolescent male must have found something terrifically adult
about this kind of writing. Of course, at fourteen I also thought the
narrator just a means to an end, a way of getting to the real story of
Kid Roberts, whose actual name is the phony-sounding Kane
Halliday. The truth is that the narrator is more likable and more

interesting than his high-born hitter. Kane Halliday is that stock
character in popular novels of the period, "the Gentleman"—
noble as the day is long, a defender of women, a dutiful son, a
boon companion, and as brave a man as ever fastened on a pair of
spats. In short, the Kid's a snore.

At fourteen, however, I must have admired him enormously.
In fact, it says something that thirty-five years later I could be
disappointed at hearing him say: "When I first went into this
game, I made up my mind that under no circumstances would I
ever step into a ring with a colored man. Never mind my reasons—
they're ethical and my own." But the Kid does fight a black man
because "a real champion should bar *no* one, whether it be a
contest of brains or brawn."

A little of this kind of rhetoric goes a long way, though never
toward making a character likable. Halliday sounds like a caffein-
ated Edward Everett Horton, but without the grace to look foolish
while declaiming on this or that outrage. Witwer may have been
giving his audience what it expected from someone who had all the
advantages except knowing what life was all about, but the Kid's
formal speech grates rather than amuses. Speaking of speaking, an
irony almost too good to be true is that a few years after the novel's
publication, an actual boxer appeared on the scene—Gene Tun-
ney by name—who, tough enough to outpoint Jack Dempsey
twice, resorted, especially when the press was around, to loony
locutions that he regarded as college speak.

Will I now go on to read or reread Witwer's thirteen other
novels, including *Fighting Back,* the sequel to *The Leather Pushers?* Probably not, though *From Baseball to Bosches* and *The Classics in Slang* make for tempting titles. My search, after all, is over. I
have my book and I've read it too. And I learned something. I
learned that Kid Roberts didn't actually like to fight; he fought
because his father made some unsound investments and lost the
family fortune. Nor, as it turns out, did Dad disapprove of his son's

profession; in fact, he got a kick out of it. As for the beautiful, classy young woman, a senator's daughter, even she rooted for the big educated palooka when he stepped between the ropes. Oh, it was Yale the Kid went to, not . . .—I mean, a heavyweight champion from Harvard? Come on.

So memory has been corrected. But there is more than a tinge of melancholy in such emendation. Neither the book nor its youthful reader exists for the other as they did on first meeting. *The Leather Pushers* is dated, longwinded, not without its dull patches. The same might be said of its middle-aged reader. But something else can be said as well. For just a few minutes while paging through the novel, I sensed through the haze of years and the intellectual veil lowered by critics and well-intentioned professors what it was like to read as if there were no tomorrow. The pure joy of reading may never be regained, but if we're lucky we can chance across one of those "good bad books" we read thirty or forty years ago and recall what it's like to be a child who reads. Such books are like old snapshots taken at the age when the baby fat is just swimming off the bone, when the personality is just beginning to acknowledge what it will find forever interesting, when the eyes begin to reveal for the first time the person who will be using them for the rest of his life.

[1997]

3

Stop the Presses:
A Petition for Less Writing

———

A point of information for those with time on their hands: if you were to read 135 books a day, every day, for a year, you wouldn't finish all the books published annually in the United States. Now add to this figure, which is upward of 50,000, the 100 or so literary magazines; the scholarly, political and scientific journals (there are 142 devoted to sociology alone), as well as the glossy magazines, of which bigger and shinier versions are now spawning, and you'll appreciate the amount of lucubration that finds its way into print. But to really get an idea of the literary glut, you have to be in it: at a convention of the American Booksellers Association or Modern Language Association, where, amid myriad displays and stalls of books, trade and academic publishers hawk their wares.

Of the many thousands of titles featured at these literary galas, only a few will turn a profit. The rest, as Calvin Trillin put it, have "a shelf life somewhere between butter and yogurt." And since many of these books are addressed to specific audiences—those who watch their weight, horoscopes, or investments—the general reading public never even learns of their existence. This still leaves, however, a daunting array of books, both factual and fictional, dealing with matters of general interest, whose numbers are calculable, many, and increasing. In 1988, for example, the Book-of-the-Month Club received 5,000 submissions, presumably only a sample of eligible books publishers culled from their lists. The printed word flourishes. Books may not be the "hot" medium that films and music are supposed to be, but publishers don't seem to be suffering from frostbite either.

As one leafs through these miscellaneous books, a surprising fact emerges: most are competently written. The other thing one soon notices is that very few rise above mere competence. To focus only on fiction and poetry, how many, by common consent, are indispensable, works without which a truer understanding of contemporary life and art could not be obtained? And if one accepts the idea of a canon, which books actually stand a chance of admission? Good books abound, pretty good books are routine, great books are not only scarce, they don't seem to be expected anymore. Is it possible that the absence of greatness is a function of books' multiplicity? I, for one, believe that it is. And so, a modest proposal: let's cut back on this furious literary activity and limit the numbers to a reasonable amount.

The complaint of there being too many books—never mind their quality—is nothing new. It stretches back almost as far as writing itself. In "The Burden of the Past and the English Poet," W. Jackson Bate quotes an Egyptian scribe, Khakheperresenb (about 2000 B.C.): "Would I had phrases that are not known, utterances that are strange, in new language that has not been used." And which utterances, one must wonder, got on the nerves of the author of Ecclesiastes (traditionally King Solomon, about 950 B.C.): "Of making many books there is no end"? Among the truly pious, of course, all books but one were superfluous, distractions from God's word as revealed in His Testaments, which is why Martin Luther decreed that the "multitude of books is a great evil." (Of course, Luther himself could not resist participating in extending the evil.)

Most expressions of unhappiness with books come from those who write them. Robert Burton, author of *The Anatomy of Melancholy*, a book that draws heavily on other books, looked around him in 1620 and saw a pack of "illiterate scribblers," possessed by "an incurable itch for writing." Two centuries later, William Hazlitt remarked plaintively: "When we have Shakespear, we do not want more Shakespear; one Milton, one Pope or Dryden, is enough. . . . Who has seen all the fine paintings, or read all the fine poetry, that already exist—and yet till we have done this what do we want with more?" But evermore, as Poe's Raven might miscroak, keep coming. And writers keep lamenting. In their popular *Elements of Style* (1959), William Strunk and E. B. White note that the "volume of writing is enormous, these days, and much of it has a sort of wordiness about it, almost as though the author were in a state of euphoria. 'Spontaneous me,' sang Whitman, and in his innocence let loose the hordes of uninspired scribblers who would one day confuse spontaneity with genius."

If we were to leave it at this, the constancy of the complaint could be said to work against it. If it was ever thus, even when there were relatively few books around, why worry about numbers? And just how many books *are* we talking about? Although exact figures cannot be cited, since so many books were lost over the centuries, it is believed that King Ramses II (the Ozymandias of Shelley's poem), who died in 1225 B.C., had about 20,000 papyrus rolls in his palace at Thebes (one work covered anywhere from one to one hundred rolls). The Assyrian ruler Assurbanipal (reigned 669–26 B.C.) owned 10,000 different works on 30,000 clay tablets the size of small pillows (an average tablet being equivalent to two or three modern pages), and the great library at

Alexandria may have contained at one time nearly 700,000 papyrus and parchment rolls.

Most of these early "books" were actually records of government, temple, and private transactions. Eventually, they were supplemented by treatises on medicine, agriculture, law, geography, astronomy, and religion. By 300 B.C. private libraries were common among wealthy Greeks, and about one thousand authors lived during Greece's classical period. Later, there were clearly enough inspired Romans around to warrant Pliny's exclamation: "What a company of poets has this year brought out!"

After the fall of Rome, many ancient texts found their way to the Arab world. The royal library at Córdoba in A.D. 800 possessed some 400,000 volumes, and it was said of one Baghdad scholar that it required "four hundred camel loads" to transport his books. In Europe, however, books were not so easily had, as is apparent from the size of private and university libraries. The Sorbonne library in 1289 owned about 1,100 books, and Oxford's Oriel College a paltry 100 as late as 1375. As for private libraries, the most famous belonged to Richard de Bury, Bishop of Durham, who in the fourteenth century amassed 1,500 volumes.

All this changed, of course, with the introduction of movable type in Europe in 1436. In the sixteenth century alone, 100,000 different books were printed, and by the time typesetting machines were perfected in the late nineteenth century, books were coming into and going out of print with such regularity that it became impossible to keep track of them. Today the number of extant books can at best be approximated. According to the 1988 *Bowker Annual,* the Library of Congress's collection at present consists of 85,895,835 "items," including catalogued titles, nonclassified printed matter, manuscripts, and microfilm. Now that's one hell of a lot of camel loads.

Notwithstanding the complaint's longevity, numbers do have consequences: they affect the perception of the thing they enumerate. Quality, as diamond merchants know, is a condition of quantity. For this reason alone, one might worry that too much gets written and too much is written about what gets written. Who reads—who could read—all this stuff?

A proper response might be: what do you care? If writers want to write and publishers publish, what business is it of yours? Put this way, any justification will most likely sound both pompous and petulant. To answer, one can only fall back on a personal concern. For someone who reads as a matter of course, for whom books, despite the critics' polemics, are still the truest expressions of the human condition, there is a fundamental need to scan, savor, and study words on a printed page. But more and more, the printed page is treated like a commodity, something to be bought, used, and discarded, something whose identity is bound up with the publishing industry's advertising campaigns.

However, there's more to it than just one reader's anxieties. The exponential increase in books has broad implications for readers and literature alike. Back in 1819, Washington Irving was already brooding: "The stream of literature has swollen into a torrent—augmented into a river—expanded into a sea. . . . It will soon be the employment of a lifetime merely to learn [books'] names. Many a man of passable information at the present day reads scarcely anything but reviews, and before long, a man of erudition will be little better than a mere walking catalogue." If I am any indication, Irving's fears were well founded. There are dozens of novels by Balzac, Conrad, Mann, and others whose titles and subjects I'm familiar with but which I have not read. What's more, I'll probably never get around to them, and my excuse is that there just isn't enough time.

The problem of numbers, by definition, also figures into the problem of canon-making or, rather unmaking. Which novels, plays, and poems belong, and which do not? One way, of course, of resolving the problem is to dismantle the canon itself. Readers who have cut their teeth on the classics, however, do not fret over which books are worthy and which are not. George Steiner, acknowledging both literary abundance and literary value, is not put off: "There are more than 'a hundred great books,' more than a thousand. But their number is not inexhaustible." Perhaps not, but that number, whatever it may be, is also probably unreachable.

Another problem: since numbers conceal better than they reveal, how can good books stand out from the rest? One solution is offered by George Gissing in *New Grub Street*. He writes: "The struggle for existence among books is nowadays so severe as among men. If a writer has friends connected with the press, it is the plain duty of those friends to do their utmost to help him. What matter if they exaggerate, or even lie? The simple, sober truth has no chance whatever of being listened to and it is only by volume of shouting that the ear of the public is held." Sounds like the survival of the loudest—and it also sounds all too familiar. Publishers drop huge litters, and books climb over each other, vying for attention. But even if such tactics succeed, readers may well become disillusioned by books' repeated failure to live up to their billing.

I'm not suggesting that works of literary merit are no longer being written or noticed; what I am saying is that books are so commonplace that a truly good one seems no more significant than a truly bad one. There seems to be nothing special about books; certainly we do not await books with the same eagerness that a compact and homogeneous reading public awaited novels by Hugo or Dickens and poetry by Tennyson or Hardy. In 1858, Longfellow's *Courtship of Miles Standish* sold 10,000 copies in London in a single day. If a book now creates a stir, it's usually not because of its literary value but because it's tied to celebrity or scandal, or, more recently, because an ayatollah has put a price on the author's head. Masterpieces may still be stitched together, but could any one novel or poem today have the critical impact of Eliot's *Waste Land* (1922)? For what it's worth, there were 758 fiction titles, excluding poetry, published in 1922; in 1988, there were 7,674.

Not that every book has to be a masterpiece. One reads, after all, for a variety of reasons—pleasure, curiosity or simply to pass the time. Spinoza and Goethe are fine fellows, but on some days only Raymond Chandler or P. G. Wodehouse will do. The mystery or romance does not constitute a threat to literature; it is rather all the overhyped books that claim our attention at the expense of the great books of the past—and the present. The issue is obviously complicated by various social, economic, and technological forces, but surely this multitude of books has the inevitable effect of canceling out individual voices.

Needless to say, one cannot prove the trivializing effect of endless books. By the same token, who can blame conscientious readers for feeling demoralized by these overbearing numbers? Indeed, one might even be forgiven for thinking about ways to make these numbers a bit more humble. Censorship? Perish the thought. A regulatory board to review manuscripts before publication? A bit dicey. Who would sit in judgment? Who'd guard the guardians?

Evidently, such democratic niceties didn't trouble Montaigne in 1588: "But there should be some legal restraint aimed against inept and useless writers as there is against vagabonds and idlers. Both I and a hundred others would be banished from the hands of our people. This is no jest. Scribbling seems to be a sort of symptom of an unruly age."

What age isn't unruly? No, legal measures are out. Writers can't be forced to desist from writing. But can they be talked into it? Two thousand years ago, the Roman poet Horace recommended that writers wait nine years before publishing their work, just to make sure it holds up. Most writers, of course, do not have this luxury; contracts must be honored and bills paid. Moreover, that necessary egotism or naïveté that underwrites poetry and fiction is not put off by a book's slim chance of winning renown. The fact of being in print is reward enough. For though books may be a dime a dozen, if an aspiring writer's name is Dickensen, his or her book may one day end up on a shelf touching spines with *Bleak House*.

Perhaps, then, this incentive can be used against itself. If more writers suffered from old Khakheperresenb's anxiety of influence, fewer might take up pens against a sea of precursors. The obvious protest that artists cannot be shackled to or inhibited by the past only begs the question. For it's a Panglossian critic who maintains that our postmoderns have charted waters unvisited by our moderns; and for all the lip service paid to the Poundian dictum of making it new, there is precious little that is new, and a precious lot that's not.

I'd be a fool to think that writers will take my petition for less writing seriously. I doubt even that many readers share my feelings. The myth of the dedicated, downtrodden artist waging his lonely struggle against an indifferent society still exerts a powerful sway. Our sympathy goes to those trying to create, not to those calling for a creative slowdown. Nevertheless, this is not a bad time for writers to live in. Despite stories about slush piles and rejection slips, it's easier than ever before to get published. There were— think of it—25,900 publishers in the United States in 1988. True, most are of the mom-and-pop variety, releasing only two or three titles a year (sometimes the same two or three titles), but surely somewhere out there is a small press or little magazine with a quirky one-word name that will find your style interesting, your thoughts profound, and your point of view unique.

None of this is meant to suggest that writers outside Hollywood get rich. Most just manage to scrape by, but they do get by.

According to the Authors Guild, the median income for writers in 1988 was almost $8,000. Not a princely sum, but many writers were able to parlay a novel or a few strategically placed poems and short stories into grants, readings, panel discussions, and teaching stints. Writers, too, know how to "network."

No, it's not writers I feel sorry for, but the fruits of their labors: the accumulated pages that wait untouched, unread, unknown in libraries and secondhand bookstores around the world. Every year, according to *Books in Print,* another 70,000 titles go out of print; and among them, undoubtedly, are buried worthwhile books. Does anyone care about this besides St. Jerome, the patron saint of libraries? Or has he too finally broken down and bought himself a VCR?

It's hopeless, I know, but perhaps writers might think twice and ask themselves: do I *have* to write this book? Will the world be better for what I write? Wouldn't everyone, including me, be happier if I were in another line of work? Failing that, perhaps they'll simply take pity on us. We have enough to read for a while.

[1989]

4

What Do You Know?
What Don't You Know?

Emerging from the lobby of the Metropolitan Opera House one evening, I overheard one middle-aged opera-goer ask another, "Have you heard of a writer named Tolstoy, he was Russian?" I didn't catch the reply because I had come to a full stop, and by the time my mouth closed, the men had disappeared. I related the incident to a few friends and then forgot about it. Some months later I heard myself saying that it was probably unnecessary to identify the author of *The Sorrows of Young Werther* in the pages of a national magazine. The magazine's associate editor disagreed. When I suggested that most people know who wrote the novel, she replied testily that *she* didn't know. Empathic to a fault, I got the feeling that she didn't care for me or for the implication that she should have known.

A touchy subject, knowledge. Conceptually, it is almost impossible to define; and as a practical matter, a condition of factual awareness, what constitutes core or essential knowledge? Just what is it we're supposed to know? "Now, what I want is Facts," insists the schoolmaster Thomas Gradgrind in *Hard Times*. "Teach these boys and girls nothing but Facts. Plant nothing else, and root out everything else. . . . In this life, we want nothing but Facts, sir; nothing but Facts."

There, I have just summoned the ghost of two more facts: the author of *Hard Times* (Charles Dickens) and his low opinion of pedagogy in the person of Gradgrind. Should you have known this? Deep thinking or high imagining is not required to answer. Like Gradgrind, I want the facts, or more precisely the data that I'm responsible for knowing. "Just the facts," Jack Webb rapped out on *Dragnet* (an allusion that opens a whole new can of facts).

In 1987, E. D. Hirsch, Jr., assisted by science writer James Trefil and historian Joseph Kett, published *Cultural Literacy: What Every American Needs to Know.* The book, reprinted many times, includes an updated appendix of "5,000 essential names, phrases, dates, and concepts" that Trefil identifies as "What Literate Americans Know." Arranged alphabetically—*Robert's Rules of Order;* Robeson, Paul; Robinson, Jackie; rob Peter to pay Paul; rococo; Rodgers and Hammerstein—the items, to say the least, make an eclectic group. Despite my harrumphing over a few of these "essential" facts (why Bizet, Georges, but not Berlioz, Hector?), I have no problem with the list, since the authors go out of their way to stress its provisional nature. The list is *descriptive* rather than *prescriptive* (their italics), illustrating the range and character of knowledge, not its beginning or end.

Where do the items come from? Apparently they are culled from the general print media, where they appear without explanation, leading Hirsch to suppose that they represent "the information actually possessed by literate Americans." Hirsch tends to refer to these facts as background knowledge or wide-ranging background information or, more pointedly, as the *shared* knowledge of literate Americans. He also believes this background knowledge to be "necessary for functional literacy and effective national communication." Well, yes, but isn't there something pat in this shifting from what every American should know to what literate Americans actually do know? Not only am I not persuaded that every American should know what's on the list, I am not so sure that the list really suggests what most literate Americans do know.

Cultural Literacy received the glowing (some might say glowering) endorsement of former Secretary of Education William Bennett and other conservative pundits. Properly gratified, Hirsch also knew that such august benediction could put liberals off the book's thesis, which, in brief, finds a net loss in shared knowledge. If Hirsch is right to fret over this knowledge drain, he is rather optimistic in putting so much stock in what education may ultimately achieve. Functional literacy and effective national communication are no guarantors of decency or moral rectitude. Indeed, it strikes me that if the argument needs to be made, the cause is already lost. When Matthew Arnold defined culture as "a pursuit of our total perfection by means of getting to know, on all the matters which most concern us, the best which has been thought and said in the world," he was not bringing a new idea into the world, nor was he proselytizing for universal education. He was simply reminding his readers of what they already knew: knowledge helps people to live. When Hirsch says much the same thing, a whiff of desperation clings to the page.

This brings me to the subtext of Hirsch's thesis, a troubling component of general ignorance that Hirsch seems reluctant to say out loud. Namely: many people today couldn't care less about not knowing things. Information, if not pertinent to life or career, simply doesn't matter to most people. You can't argue with the facts, but you can ignore or dismiss them. People do. In point of fact, there is a growing resistance to facts: from boardrooms to cocktail bars, educated and well-read people, people who would characterize themselves as informed, are simply unrepentant about not knowing things that do not reflect their interests. No one is claiming that ignorance is bliss, but few are apologizing for it.

Indeed, ignorance of facts has taken on the neutrality of fact itself, sloughing off any stigma of intellectual abdication.

I dwell on this because it doesn't jibe with what I remember. Thirty years ago, when I unpacked my bags at a large midwestern university, the classroom was not yet neutral ground where teachers were loath to demand results or to discipline the unprepared. If my own trepidation reflected a wider anxiety, difficult questions were like flares that lit up the inattentive or benighted and left them squirming in their seats. More to the point, a rough or disadvantaged childhood didn't get you off the hook. Sure, there were reasons for gaps in one's education, but gaps they were. Ignorance could be explained, ignorance could even be justified, but—and this is a "but" that throbs with portent—ignorance was wrong. Somewhere along the line, you had slipped through the system; it may not have been your fault, but the ultimate responsibility was yours.

So what happened between then and now? Whence came the defiance required to face down facts, to regard with impunity what formerly was part of a traditional humanities education? A number of possible explanations come to mind: the decline of literacy; the ascendancy of technology; the recondite nature of modern science and the increasing specialization of all disciplines, including the humanities; the fall of the public intellectual and "man of letters"; the difficulty of texts that seek to explain why reading is so darned difficult; the popularization (and concomitant simplification) of "great" writers; and the fact that many educators have no problem with putting quotation marks around the word *great,* even when referring to Shakespeare.

Other suspects may be hauled in and interrogated, but the underlying cause, the shadowy perpetrator, remains at large. An intellectual attitude has no cause; it floats in, soft on the heels of a series of cultural events and trends, and becomes part of the regular interchange between school and society. Making a positive ID even more difficult is that the attitude in question is less transgressive than expressive. License not to know is not the same thing as rebelling against an existing body of knowledge (though the equation may exist retroactively). But if the cause is elusive, the effect is not. When was the last time someone's saying "What, you never heard of so-and-so?" put you off your feed, made you feel a tad inadequate?

Inadequacy, of course, can be rectified; the real problem is knowing whether one actually *is* inadequate where knowledge is concerned. Express dismay that I don't know the title of the latest self-help book, the name of the hot new rock band, the CEO of some huge corporation, the capital of Mississippi, and my head remains high. Not my bailiwick, I respond cheerily. I don't need to know that.

Then again, I'm not entirely sure what I do need to know. I have a general idea, but if you ask me to outline the parameters of knowledge, I may start off briskly but in short order stumble, vacillate, hedge. Like most liberal arts majors, I have made my peace with the two cultures and figure that about 70 percent of scientific fact is outside my competence curve. But this still leaves a rather intimidating amount of information inside the arc. To narrow it further, let us assume that most people who consider themselves cultivated, if that word still has currency, equate knowledge with recognizing significant historical individuals, trends, and events. While business, science, economics, mathematics, engineering, and law are not to be sneezed at, the pervasive impression exists that these subjects by themselves do not have the intellectual cachet associated with art, literature, music, and history.

Now we're getting somewhere. Or are we? The implication that knowing the historical highlights confers real knowledge on anyone would find little support in the academic community. The very idea of highlights—a string of books, artworks, events, and ideas, the nucleus of the traditional liberal arts education—has been under attack for just about the number of years that I have been out of school. Western Civilization courses (a.k.a. "From Plato to NATO") are shriveling up under the sanctimonious glare of Cultural Studies. In many cases, the study of the Great Books (and Great Individuals) has been supplemented or even supplanted by the study of the more "ordinary" lives, works, and occupations of hitherto unrecognized people.

In the postmodern classroom, knowledge itself has undergone a bizarre makeover. Once associated with the mental constructs either innate or issuing from data presented by the senses, knowledge with a capital K now smacks of elitism, bounded by cultural exigencies and manipulated by those with the power to do so— i.e., those pesky privileged dead white European males. Students are urged to get hip to what "knowledge" and "culture" really signify: the power struggle between classes, races, and sexes. Who is privileged to call the shots, to decide what's important to know and what is not? In other words, you don't have to know what a liberal elitist cabal has shoved down your throat.

If you buy into this, you are free to pick and choose among whatever does not offend. Or—if you know something about the ways of academia—you can take this "dissing" of knowledge with a grain of salt and continue, guilt-free, to believe that civilization in the West, as in the East, presents a chain of events, consisting of both word and deed, the interpretation of which is fluid, but without which one cannot begin to understand how the end of the second millennium came to have the shape and temper it has. In which case you have no choice but to learn, commit to memory, and juggle the facts as you find them. Despite what theory-minded professors advocate, what we are talking about is *more* information, not radically different information, and despite the impediment of theory, anyone with a strong stomach for thick linguistic stew can digest Adorno, Foucault, Derrida, Lacan, and Bakhtin just as readers once had to swallow Kant, Hegel, Heidegger, Merleau-Ponty, and the like.

So have we come to an understanding of the parameters of knowledge? Hardly. Knowledge is an odd business, dependent on our expectations and biases. That someone does not know Tolstoy seems like a pretty astonishing lapse to me. But consider *who* did not know: a middle-aged white individual attending an opera in New York City. Had the speaker been a twenty-year-old African-American sitting on a stoop in Harlem, or a small-town garage attendant in Kansas, would I have been surprised? No more so than many college teachers around the country whose incoming freshman classes, with the exception of a few enterprising self-starters, have never head of Homer or Dante.

As for the college-educated editor unaware of *Werther*'s creator—well, why should she have known? Goethe has as much relevance to her as Hecuba had to Hamlet's friend the player. (Does the name *Hecuba* ring any bells?) At some point, the quick recall of untrammeled facts degenerates into entertainment, a contest, a way of earning money on *Jeopardy*. But that does not invalidate the knowledge to be gained from a liberal arts education. Whether such knowledge will greatly benefit society, as Hirsch and Company believe, or close the division between the intellectual haves and have-nots, is a question for someone else to answer.

My own sense of things is that while the chasm between those with an education and those whom society has hindered from getting one has certainly been bridged, with access to knowledge now open to all classes and ethnic groups, the outcome is still less than perfect. Nothing like a uniform education exists for all those who seek to learn, and far too many college graduates emerge speaking different languages, even within the humanities. When

one person's intellectual bread and butter is another person's ar-
cana, something is wrong. If the syllables "Tol-stoy" elicit no
recognition, what vast regions of literary blankness must lie outside our centers of learning?

The trick, of course, is to determine the set of cultural facts
that educated people can agree on. But how does one go about
planning the itinerary? The very thought is enough to make us pull
up, because when you get down to it, this is nothing more than a
whistle-stop tour of the high points. Undeterred, the expatriate
critic George Steiner warned back in 1965: "Not to know Melville
or Rimbaud, Dostoyevsky or Kafka, not to have read Mann's
Doktor Faustus or Pasternak's *Doctor Zhivago* is a disqualification
so severe from the notion of a vital literacy that we must raise, if not
answer, the entire question of whether the close study of one
literature makes good sense."

Although some readers may find Steiner's exhortation perfectly sound, others may balk at having to read *Doktor Faustus*. Or
one may agree with Steiner in principle but decide that "a vital
literacy" can be achieved without learning another language or
even reading *Doctor Zhivago* in translation. A vital literacy, like
knowledge itself, is not to be conveniently framed. We may know
(sort of) where it begins: the Bible, Plato, Chaucer, Shakespeare,
Milton—but where does it end? Pythagoras is a familiar name, but
what of Protagoras? One may have read Goethe and Schiller, but
not Klopstock. Or Kleist. Or Landor. Or Cowley. Sooner or later,
a name, a book, a historical fact will blindside you, and you may
well wonder, "Should I have known that?"

Calling attention to the signposts that might let us proceed
further, Edward Hirsch has marshaled his five thousand facts, and
more recently Harold Bloom's *Western Canon* arrived flourishing
not one but four "appendixes" of canonical authors and their
works. A sampling of Bloom's essential writers includes Snorri
Sturluson, Tirso de Molina, Samuel Daniel, George Etherege,

Maurice Scève, John Galt, Adalbert Stifter, Trumbull Stickney, and Jones Very. I don't know about you, but my ego is doing a little stutter step trying to recover its balance.

True, one can walk safely into most faculty lounges *sans* John Galt, but to take comfort in this is to exhibit the same defensive posture adopted by the editor who didn't know (and didn't care) who had written *The Sorrows of Young Werther.* In light of Hirsch's descriptive items and Bloom's prescriptive list, one has to wonder if there is a rung on the intellectual ladder from which we can look around and maintain that we know enough. Is it enough to have read, say, four or five novels by Balzac and not the entire oeuvre? Is it okay to know the name John Galsworthy without having plowed through *The Forsyte Saga?* Do you move up a rung if you saw it on PBS? At what point does familiarity with a subject turn into expertise?

A rather prosaic phenomenon attends a person's own cache of knowledge. One's regard for, one's opinion of, certain facts depends pretty much on whether they are already part of one's repertoire. Did I know the name Thomas De Quincey? someone asked me recently. I did, as it happens, and thought the questioner, a former English major, should have known as well. Why did I feel this way? Because De Quincey's *Confessions of an English Opium-Eater* has been in my memory bank for twenty-five years, that's why.

Coming across an unfamiliar tidbit, our initial response is often: Well, how important can this person, event, or book be if *I* haven't heard of it? The worst offenders are those who have a passing acquaintance with books, who have read a lot and *think* they have read a lot. Someone like me, for example. And it is precisely people like me who need to get their faces slapped once in a while with names or facts we have never heard of and whose existence others regard as self-evident.

Leafing through a copy of the *Times Literary Supplement,* I

came across a review of *The Correspondence of Thomas Warton,*
edited by David Fairer. I didn't know the first thing about Thomas
Warton and, naturally, knowing nothing, I felt that it was all right
not to know. Hey, if Warton were important, I'd already know all
about him, wouldn't I? It gets worse. As I scanned the review, by
one David Wormersley, I learned that Warton was Professor of
Poetry at Oxford (1757–1767), Poet Laureate (1785), and the first
historian of English literature. Bad enough as it is that I didn't
know this guy, I also had to read Wormersley's casual aside that the
"conclusion of [Dr.] Johnson's letter to Warton of December 21,
1754, in which he expressed his enduring sense of bereavement
after the death of his wife two years before, is well known." Well
known, huh? Then, after quoting the relevant part of the letter,
Wormersley comments: "Most will have read this passage in the
editions of Johnson's letters by Chapman, and, more recently,
Redford."

The assumption is staggering if Wormersley, a Fellow of Jesus
College, Oxford, believes he is addressing a generally literate au-
dience, as opposed to specialists in eighteenth-century studies.
I'm not sure what percentage of *TLS* readers know the name of
Thomas Warton or could tell you much, if anything, about him.
But that is me speaking—that is, a person for whom Warton could
not be terribly important because he knew nothing about him.
Wormersley would find me woefully, culpably ignorant—and he
would be right.

Having now learned a little about Warton, I imagine that he
had few doubts about what constituted a vital literacy. Warton
lived in a century when a man of learning in one thing was a man of
learning in all things, when a consummate familiarity with all that
had been written and thought was considered both a proper and a
reasonable goal. Indeed, at the beginning of the eighteenth century, the French economist A. R. J. Turgot claimed that it was
possible to discern "every shade of barbarism and refinement . . .

every step taken by the human mind, the likeness of every stage through which it has passed." Such confidence was, of course, made possible by an educational system in which a clearly defined set of cultural standards held sway. An aspiring scholar didn't choose what to learn; he simply made his way to the common source, the Book—from which all knowledge flowed—and drank as much as he could hold.

As for the argument that in Warton's time there was less to know—that, intellectually speaking, things were on a smaller scale—how do we make a neat or manageable bundle of the social, religious, aesthetic, philological, and scientific schemes, doctrines, and speculations that were then flourishing contemporaneously? In philosophy alone, Cartesianism, Berkeleian idealism, Kantean epistemology, Lockean empiricism, and Humean skepticism caromed off one another even as they were being enlisted in the service of Orientalism, pietism, Newtonian mechanism, nationalism, and the place of *Volkspoesie* in society. A dense forest of facts and ideas had sprung up in England, Germany, and France by the end of the eighteenth century, and yet the author of *Werther* felt no compunction about characterizing a person unable to give a complete accounting of the past three thousand years as someone who lived a superficial life, who lived, in fact, in darkness.

The problem, it bears repeating, is not so much one of difficulty as it is one of lowered expectations. Most people today don't think they know everything, but they probably feel they know what they're supposed to know. Scientist, lawyer, teacher, stockbroker, machinist, doctor, or editor—our hubris is such that each of us measures important knowledge by our portion of it. (Incidentally, the fellow who wrote that man is the measure of all things was Protagoras.) From within this self-imposed, self-enclosed intellectual habitat, one may regard the world of (others') knowledge with enviable disinterest.

Nor is scholarship itself immune from the feeling that there are

restrictions on what is possible to know. In *Defenders of the Text,*
Anthony Grafton marks the difference in how pre-Renaissance and
post-Renaissance interpreters of classical literature went about their
tasks. The Scholastics read by testing logical and rhetorical stresses
and tensions, whereas Renaissance and Enlightenment humanists
endeavored to understand the text from the perspective of the person who wrote it. The "serious effort to obtain that sort of knowledge," says Grafton, "became the first characteristically modern
form of intellectual life. Such knowledge, moreover, lurked in the
details of the ancient texts."

Details?—which details? Scholars studying the work of forgotten scholars were probably not troubled by such a piddling
question. Nevertheless, once it emerged that there was something
or some things that *were supposed* to be known in order to understand what happened, knowledge became problematic. Indeed, in
the very claims made for a complete accounting, one might discern
the first stirring of doubt as to the efficacy of such an undertaking.
New facts have a way of turning up and turning into more facts:
important, verging on important, trivial. The more degrees and
gradations of knowledge we recognize, the more potential facts
swim into our ken; influences and relationships multiply, and
the whole thing soon becomes ridiculously complicated. How can
we possibly know everything when we can't be sure what should
be known?

To ask the question does not necessarily mean that the search
is futile. To put it bluntly, the course of human events has been
shaped by art, anatomy, religion, politics, science, geography, ex-
ploration, trade, accident, and catastrophe. Some men and some
women, some inventions, some events, some works of literature
and art have had a greater impact than others. Why say otherwise?
There is, after all, a forceful distinction to be made between not
knowing Copernicus and Columbus and being a scholarly pig
snuffling for intellectual truffles. The possession of knowledge

does not depend on the ability to recognize *every* person or event, but on the awareness that it requires a foundation on which the ladder may start. Or we may read the story of mankind as rings of growth in a tree, or layers of wash on a rock, with speckles of color showing through successive rings or coats, some fading, others reappearing.

D isputing the idea that the dead writers are remote from us because we know so much more than they did, T. S. Eliot famously countered: "Precisely, and they are that which we know." I'm not so sure. With the exception of a few noted men of letters, we do not know the dead writers, and if we do, it's a toss-up whether we know more than they did. Whenever I go back to Montaigne, Robert Burton, and Samuel Johnson, it occurs to me that they knew more than I do now, despite my knowing them.

As the past recedes and the dead writers stay dead, it and they become less real, less essential somehow, and their remoteness seems to be accelerating (if such a thing is possible) at an alarming pace. Not only has high culture been knocked off its pedestal, the pedestal itself has been kicked aside. It's not simply that the canon has been deracinated; what really distinguishes the past few decades is the reversal of numbers between the old facts and the new, between the classic and the contemporary. Increasingly, more of the new is being required, and less of the old. John Dryden hasn't been dropped in favor of John Milton; both are dropped to make room for Stephen King.

No offense to Mr. King, but is there any good reason I should know his name in the name of education? For that matter, there are many things I now know that I'd just as soon not—the names L. Ron Hubbard, John Wayne Bobbitt, Howard Stern, and Steely Dan; the words to half a dozen rock songs ("Hey, hey, you, you, get offa my cloud"); the salaries paid to certain basketball players; and

a thousand other trivial odds and ends that the media as well as
friends and acquaintances keep stuffing into my mental chamber.

Arthur Conan Doyle, in the voice of Sherlock Holmes, once
likened the mind to an attic, a storeroom requiring the occasional
clearing out in order to make room for more information. If that is
the case, then what useful niche does Barbara Walters occupy?
What important fact has she replaced or is she keeping out? Most
likely the mental attic can comfortably hold all the junk we can lug
up, but there is something to be said for deciding what is well
made, well thought out, or notable in the story of mankind, and
thus best learned and best remembered.

Ignorance may not be a sin, but it isn't defensible either. One
can be jaunty as hell about what one doesn't know, but does this
suggest anything but a temperamental disinclination toward learning? Indifference doesn't cut it as a justifiable attitude; it's part of
the same defensiveness characteristic of educators for whom
knowledge is not beholden to arbitrary standards established by
dead white European males. Nor does a changing parade of significance exempt one from learning about those individuals or works
that bring up the rear.

The objections to this unreconstructed approach to learning
are as obvious as they are predictable. Yes, things *are* more complicated than I've made them out to be; and yes, there is an awful
lot to read, and it is not always clear which books have the best
claim on our attention. All the same, you have to begin somewhere, and provided that you bring along intellectual curiosity and
a willingness to trip up every so often, it doesn't take long to realize
that information overload and specialization do not constitute in-
surmountable obstacles. If you don't know something, fine. La-
cunae may be excused (in fact, they're to be expected), but not the
attitude that fosters them. In truth, no one wears ignorance well.
It's like going out with holes in your clothes. There's nothing

plucky or smart or politically correct about not knowing the facts—any facts.

Despite the lengthening and broadening of history, each generation continues to toss up its share of polymaths, those on whom nothing, or very little, of a bookish nature is lost. Milton was supposedly such a person, as were Goethe and his contemporary Alexander von Humboldt. William James, who knew a thing or two, noted that the German scientist Ernst Mach seemed to know everything. In our own day, the science writer Jeremy Bernstein speculated that the physicist Freeman Dyson knew more about everything than he, Bernstein, knew about any one thing. Joseph Epstein, an essayist and critic, felt much the same way about the historian Arnaldo Momigliano; and it would appear from the breadth of their writings that such cultural historians as Jacques Barzun and the late Isaiah Berlin seem to have read everything that ever mattered to scholars.

The exceptions here prove no rule except the one concerning hard work, though perhaps they do suggest that a rough consensus is possible. Lists, indices, appendices are hardly the point, since putting a spotlight on certain facts leaves other facts in the shadows. What is required is respect for knowledge, a respect not contingent upon institutional criteria or expectations, but earned by intellectual grit. You must press on, you must keep learning; otherwise how will you ever realize that you have to know a lot before you can know how much you really don't know?

Not a bad goal: educated ignorance. It is but a mild paradox, one in which a healthy regard for intellectual attainment instills a proper humility before knowledge in general. It comes down to attitude. People must take it as a matter of faith that it is better to be curious about what one doesn't know than it is to be complacent about what one does know. So let's put shame back in the curriculum. Better for students and people in all walks of life to

feel abashed when unable to recognize a name, title, date, or
concept than to offer excuses for not knowing. Although one may
have cause not to know, there is no good reason for remaining in
the dark.

George Orwell said somewhere (I should try to find out
where) that by the time a man reaches the age of fifty, he has
acquired the face he deserves. One might add that he will also be
playing, more or less, with the same intellectual deck of cards
for the rest of his life. One doesn't have to be a keeper of the
intellectual flame to exhibit a healthy regard for facts. One doesn't
have to be a brain, an egghead, or a nerd to accept that no fact
is too trivial until it's been examined. In other words, one ought
to know enough not to draw any conclusions about what is enough
to know.

So should the opera-goer have heard of Tolstoy? Should the
editor have known who wrote *Werther?* Should I have been acquainted with Thomas Warton? Of course.

[1999]

5

Death, It's What Ails You

———

You who are about to read this, I salute you. Not because you're going to die any time soon, but because you *are* going to die. Maybe not today, maybe not tomorrow, but one day your day will come. Don't think I enjoy pressing your nose against the grave; it's just that I have a bone to pick with death—two hundred and six, to be precise, all of which will soon enough be picked clean by time and the elements. I'll just come out and say it: I am appalled at the prospect of my own extinction, outraged at the impending loss of someone I know so well. Now, you might think the universe minus me is no great matter, and, of course, you'd be right. In my defense, however, I should like to point out that no one remotely like me has ever been born; no one remotely like me will ever come again. Do I need to say, I am speaking of you as well?

Of course, you may be one of those happy few who don't require a salute from me: you have made your peace with mortality, or believe in a life after death, or anticipate a pleasant bonding experience with the universe. But for most of us, unless I miss my guess, death is a pretty scary proposition and something to avoid thinking about. *"Comme le soleil, la mort ne peut être regardée fixement,"* La Rochefoucauld cautioned. Then again, some can withstand the glare better than others. Personifying death, for example, softens the light ("Because I could not stop for Death / He kindly stopped for me"). And whether He sits on a pale horse with Hell following behind, or appears as a skeletal figure in hooded cloak carrying a scythe, or as a dapper Fredric March in *Death Takes a Holiday,* the message is the same: as long as *someone* shows up, there's someplace else to go.

It's religion, of course, that makes death easier to look at, as well as easier to swallow, and over the years a great deal of devotional literature has sought to reconcile people to dying. The first such books, *Ars Mariendi,* appeared in fifteenth-century Bavaria in the form of instructional pamphlets to help prep Christians for the afterlife. Given the prevalent belief that death was the doorway to eternity and that what you did here affected how you got on *there* (in one Spanish text, a single day of earthly suffering could redeem a year of purgatory time), such written aids in matters of confession, prayers, and pious bequests were promptly snapped up. From then on there has been no shortage of manuals, guides, and spiritual tracts to help us make the crossing.

It's the oldest story in the world, isn't it? At first, death is something that happens to others, never to us. Then, as the body ages, as it bends closer to the ground that will eventually receive it, death loses its accidental quality; it becomes real; it becomes close; it becomes very, very close. All the same, it's getting more and more difficult to remember. "In my day, people died," crabs an old woman in a *New Yorker* cartoon. Quite so. In centuries past, people died younger, faster, and from a greater variety of natural and unnatural causes, and they usually died at home and often lay in state where they had died. Giving birth was touch and go, and lack of sanitation, medical know-how, and proper nutrition did nothing to ensure a venerable old age, which was around sixty. That's all changed now. Technology and medical science have managed to stave off death until we reach eighty or ninety and confined the process of dying to hospitals and hospices. As a result, the pivotal event seems more of an imposition than ever, and more frightening too, now that belief in God and an afterlife has waned for so many.

If God is a story we tell ourselves, death is a story that is forced upon us; and for nearly two millennia the two stories, in a manner of speaking, completed each other. But as the link between them gradually weakened, and the deity who created death as a punishment for sin was evicted from the world, the story of death took on new meaning, or, rather, it suggested the absence of meaning entirely. In time, dying signified leaving everything and arriving nowhere; and as someone must surely have said: With the death of God, we get the birth of death—a condition of absolute nothingness. But can there be nothing, nothing at all? Advocates of UFOs claim that the absence of evidence is not evidence of absence. In the case of an afterlife, I'm afraid it is. Each of us, I wager, is a temporal hiccup, "a little gleam of time between two eternities" as Carlyle put it. And the question properly becomes: Is that so terrible? William Hazlitt evidently thought not: "There was a time when we were not: this gives us no concern—why then should it trouble us that a time will come when we shall cease to be? . . . To die is only to be as we were before we were born." Unfortunately, when writers enjoin me not to fear a state in which I cannot think or feel, I immediately think and feel that this is exactly what scares me. Philip Larkin understood this well: "Not to be here, / Not to be anywhere, / And soon; nothing more terrible, nothing more true." These lines from *Aubade,* certainly the finest modern poem on the subject, reveal a man who looked death in the face and saw only himself. Yet if *Aubade* is not exactly stoical, it is hardly plaintive: "This is a special way of being afraid / No trick dispels. . . . Death is no different whined at than withstood."

Not every writer is mordant on the subject of death. In *Darwin's Worms*, the English psychotherapist Adam Phillips enlists both Darwin and Freud to help persuade us that the only thing we have to fear is fear itself. Although readers familiar with these writers may find in Phillips's eloquent brief one too many forced-to-fit assertions about the underlying message of their work—did Darwin or Freud really "want to teach us to let time pass" or "convert us to the beauty of ephemera"?—one goes along with him when he writes that it is "the consequence, if not always the intention, of their work to make our lives hospitable to the passing of time and the inevitability of death." Phillips reminds us that death makes life precious, that without time's winged chariot hurrying near, life could not be so sweet or luminous. Well, yes. "Death is the mother of beauty," Wallace Stevens wrote, and, yes, we could not savor the moment if we didn't know that the moment would soon be gone, but from this it doesn't necessarily follow, as Phillips claims, that to love life we must come to terms with life's passing. We may think that everything worthwhile, including art and love, derives its intensity and poignancy from such knowledge, but isn't it also possible to love life without coming to terms with its passing?

Death, of course, is part of Nature's plan, and Nature, Phillips avers, is neither for nor against us; if we'd only put our ears to the ground and our trust in Darwin and Freud, we would realize that Nature is correct. And because Nature *is* always correct, Phillips proposes that "suffering is only a problem for us." He offers the following story for our approval. When asked whether he didn't think there was too much suffering in the world, the composer John Cage retorted: "No, I think there's just the right amount." Phillips likens this to smart Zen. I liken it to pure crap. Who is Cage, or anyone else for that matter, to judge what the right amount of suffering is? Let him pass a kidney stone or witness the death of his children and then say, "Ah, not a *soupçon* too much."

To be fair, by suffering Phillips means the earth's throes and heaves, its growth and decay. Taking as his model Darwin's writings on geological stirrings and organic evolution, Phillips paints Nature as a wonderful system of checks and balances in which suffering just happens. Look, he says, we can never reconcile the existence of God with the existence of evil and suffering, but if God doesn't exist, and all that exists is Nature, whose program is limited to the survival of the species, then we should be able to accept that "the idea of death saves us from the idea that there is anything to be saved from. If we are not fallen creatures, we cannot be redeemed. If we are not deluded by the wish for immortality, transience doesn't diminish us." This is nicely put, but since transience is the road to annihilation, then transience diminishes me about as far as I can be diminished, and contemplating it, while it may heighten my appreciation of life, doesn't exactly make me happy.

And Phillips wants me to be happy. No raging against the dying of the light for him. Not only does he cheerfully slam the lid down on the coffin, he also sounds at times like a secular redeemer: "When transience is not merely an occasion for mourning, we will have inherited the earth." To be honest, I'd like to believe Phillips; hell, I'd like to *be* Phillips. Temperament does not permit this. Phillips is in favor of death; I am opposed to it. Phillips brings his considerable intelligence and learning to bear on Nature and finds that Nature is bearable; I bring whatever faculties and abilities I possess to Nature only to find that Nature presents no solution for what ails me. If you're thinking that there is a right and a wrong way to view this, let me say that I am a poor example of how to meet life—and the end of life—philosophically.

There is, to be sure, a good case to be made for accepting death with an air of fatalism or detachment. In spiritual circles, it is generally believed that the more highly evolved one is, the more one feels part of a seamless web of things, a reality in which death is neither good nor bad but simply is. For Phillips, it is Nature that argues against an animus toward death; in Buddhist philosophy, it is variations on the theme of non-selfhood that smooth death's frown. In the starkest possible terms, Eastern philosophy teaches that the body and the ego are inessential trappings, and once the body, the locus of consciousness, is finished and done with, a person's true essence is released back into a receptive and harmonious universe. The idea of wholeness and continuation is also a fundamental tenet of the school of "transpersonal psychology," which considers the self already part of the whole, and therefore the "you" that expires simply goes on in another form in a slapdash marriage of Einstein and the Upanishads. Robes and incense are not required for egoless-ness. Susan Blackmore, in *Dying to Live,* which takes a skeptical look at near-death experiences, concludes with confident serenity: "I have no self and 'I' own nothing. There is no one to die. There is just this moment, and now this and now this."

Forgive me, but there *is* someone who will die, the someone who wrote those words; and I shall, up to a point, be sorry when that self gives up what it owns. Because what it owns is everything: the mind, the imagination, and the receptacle that houses them. Buddhism may instruct us to lessen our attachment to the body, but that's not so easily accomplished when one is of Nietzsche's party: "Body am I entirely, and nothing else; and soul is only a word for something about the body." It is, in fact, this confining and all-too-disposable flesh that accounts, paradoxically, for the sovereignty of the ego: the knowledge that one is unlike anyone else. Therefore, I don't care if some elemental spark of life or incorporeal part of me continues on and commingles with the composite universe. How does that compensate for the loss of Me?

> GERTRUDE: Thou know'st 'tis common; all that lives must die, /
>   passing through nature to eternity.
> HAMLET: Aye, Madam, 'tis common.
> GERTRUDE: If it be, / Why seems it so particular with thee?

That's the crux of the matter, isn't it? How can it *not* seem particular? When it comes to death, I am a cult of one, and so are
you. And when either one of us dies, the cult's membership is
decreased *in toto.* How—you may ask—does this square with
Donne's resonant *Devotions* ("No man is an island, entire of itself . . . any man's death diminishes me, because I am involved
in mankind")? Well, it doesn't, does it? And I, for one, see no
reason to conceal the fact that I feel very little empathy for people
I've never met or barely know. After all, without at least some
access to a person's interior life, whether real or imagined (as in
the case of a celebrity), it's extremely difficult to feel the loss of that
person. Surely, it is this gulf that accounts both for our acceptance
of others dying and our willingness sometimes to help them on
their way.

"I had not thought death had undone so many," says the
narrator of *The Waste Land,* echoing Dante, but referring to the
trenches of the Somme. Yes, death has undone countless many
since man first came on the scene. So many it is hard to fathom.
Stalin, a man responsible for a significant percentage of the dead
around the middle of the last century, observed: "One death is a
tragedy; a million deaths is a statistic." I have also heard it said that
there is no real difference whether nine million or ten million perish
in a war, as if there is a point beyond which numbers become
irrelevant. I disagree: there is a difference. The death of ten million
and one is greater by one than ten million. And that makes all the
difference in the world. A stranger's death may not diminish me,
but I'm damned certain that every death is significant.

For purposes of complete disclosure, let me state that not
everything I say is said with perfect confidence. Much as I'd
like to think that my obstreperous humor defines and sustains
me, there's always the chance that when my time is up I might

succumb to the temptation of belief or tranquility. All the pertinent books recount that when people fall ill and die, they pass through stages of emotional stress that eventually lead to acceptance. In transpersonal psychology, such surrender is tantamount to arriving at a higher state of consciousness, the awareness that we are about to return home. Kierkegaard said much the same thing in relation to finding God: "To let go is to lose your foothold temporarily. Not to let go is to lose your foothold forever." This letting go in order to find something greater than oneself is no doubt a good thing, but whenever I feel the urge to do so, I am restrained by William James's remark that "all religions begin with the cry 'Help.'" And belief dictated by fear simply doesn't wash.

The truth is, I don't warm to what I cannot understand. A time will come when "time and I" will cease. There will be Nothing, No Thing, only the ———. That is clearly impossible. Death, then, is the metaphysical problem par excellence, a problem that, oddly enough, does not seem to have engaged the thought of most philosophers. Although Socrates characterized philosophy as the practice of dying, and the Stoics argued that fear of death interfered with proper comportment while alive, few philosophers have grappled discursively with mortality. This reticence, however, came to a startling turnaround with the writings of Martin Heidegger. Since I am not being paid enough to reread *Being and Time,* let me just say that, for Heidegger, our consciousness of death, manifested by *angst* (dread), is essential in recovering a fundamental and uncorrupted approach to thought itself. Heidegger elevates death to a position from which existence and being are thrown into stark relief. As the presupposed goal of sentient creatures, death, or more literally our awareness of it, cuts through eternity, creating a narrow opening in which time and history carve out their meaning. It is, in fact, because of death that historical existence and individual consciousness take precedence over eternity.

What Heidegger (and Kant and Hegel before him) intended was a reformulation or inversion of priorities. The way to Truth involved recognizing the preconditions of thought, of defining the relation between the self and the self that knows itself as a self. I summarize shamelessly, but, essentially, philosophizing about death is akin to breaking down assumptions in order to determine the true priority of things. Before you can find meaning in life you must first confront the possibility that life has no meaning. Before you can rest easy you must first accept the profound uneasiness that underscores existence. The religious parallel is obvious: You cannot be found unless you first realize that you are lost. Of course, the problem with any attempt to seal in knowledge by using a cognitive glue is the very mind-body problem that sets the whole process in motion. In a sense, it's hopeless. Language and logic, which are entwined, unravel in the face of nonbeing, which has no correlative in actuality. And the true state of affairs may simply be that, once you draw breath, nonbeing is moot. "Death is not an event in life," Wittgenstein famously wrote; "we do not live to experience death."

In which case, I can envision a scenario that tones down my own aversion to death—at least, death in a general sense. I may not be ready to go, but would I undo death if I could? Say I had the ability to resurrect the corpses of people I had never met and knew nothing about. Do I automatically restore inanimate matter to life? Do I, in effect, turn nonexistence into existence? After all, I'm not doing anyone a favor since there is, at the moment, no one to do a favor for. As passionately as I choose life over death, I wonder if not being isn't preferable to being, even though it's impossible to imagine what the former state is like. Max Beerbohm remarked that he had been lucky once—when he was born. By which he meant that birth was all that was required by way of luck. Although I wouldn't have it otherwise—having been born, I mean—how many of us can say the same and mean it?

Luck may have brought us into the world, but the world itself doesn't always deal us a winning hand. Nor does thinking about our place in it necessarily increase our chances for happiness. According to Camus, anguish is the perpetual state of the lucid man in whom the thought of existence is concentrated. But for philosophers bent on systematically establishing the connection between knowing and truth, it is the very willingness to confront the idea of existence and the end of existence that gives life its meaning. The implication is both clear and severe: If one doesn't cogitate on existence, then one's own existence won't reach its full potential. I wish I could be so certain. Who exists more fully: the person who plunders the meaning of existence every waking moment or one who exists without giving the matter any thought at all? "Experience," Goethe pronounced, "is only half of experience." This may be true for those who make a point of scrutinizing their own lives, but in what sense do such people live more fully than others? Is it a conundrum without an answer or is the answer as simple as the one provided by Valéry: "Sometimes I think; and sometimes I am"?

Given this bewildering stricture, I don't see how there can be happy philosophers. The more we wrestle with existential questions, the more anxious we become, and after a while we may just want to throw up our hands. ("How I hate God and death!" wrote Joyce. "How I like Nora.") Hazlitt has something to say about this as well: "The effeminate clinging to life as such, as a general or abstract idea, is the effect of a highly civilized and artificial state of society." In Hazlitt's view, sedentary and studious men suffer from an inordinate fear of death, which can be moderated by a "life of action and danger," an approach to things that sets "a just value on life." Does this help you? It doesn't me. Just what is the right value? Apparently, intellectualizing the world is an occupational hazard, or perhaps just the consequence of not having a real occupation to begin with.

Still, Hazlitt has a point. If you are by nature of a studious or melancholic turn, your mind may turn to thoughts of death. And as a melancholic this is not something you need. So what do you do? Well, you can, as the song has it, accentuate the positive. Rejoice in the fact that you *can* think; think all day long, think about everything, including thinking; read, learn, solve problems, take up astrophysics or chess or whatever challenges the mind. Or take a page from Hazlitt (Robert Burton said this, too) and get busy, make sure the phone keeps ringing, because barring an accident, the race *is* to the swift. And half of experience can do quite nicely. You think Donald Trump worries about the meaning of life or death?

We may not all agree as to what life is or what happens after we die, but we can all agree that death defines us. Take away death and you take away what makes us human. Take away death and you stop Nature in its tracks. Nature, after all, is motion, ceaseless turmoil in ways both large and small. However stable and inert things may appear, molecules are always in flux, and, sooner or later, everything erodes, evaporates, and disappears. Life is effusion, a constant replenishing, said the French philosopher Georges Bataille, and its renewal "is possible on one condition: that the spent organisms give way to new ones." It's just not a pretty process: from death comes putrefaction, from putrefaction comes life, and the sight and stench of it go right to the heart of the matter: the heart is an organ, we are viscera and entrails, and our insides look like the insides of rats and warthogs. Worm food each and every one of us.

Somehow this unpleasantness is also, according to Bataille, at the very root of our erotic life. Apparently, the alimentary nature of sex, with its concomitant fluids and odors, is linked to the rot of death (something you may want to bear in mind the next time you're feeling randy). Sexual intercourse also has a deeper lesson: When pleasure is so pure and powerful that the ego merges with the voluptuous experience, so that the experience overwhelms the self, then rapture literally becomes you, and you are, in a manner of speaking, temporarily dead. Hence the equation of orgasm with *la petite mort.* A consummation devoutly to be wished, you might say. But I'm not so sure. Not that I don't like a good time, but if truth be told, I'm leery of ecstasy, precisely because you do disappear. It's only a little death perhaps, but it tends to remind me of its big brother.

Although I expect I am not alone in my fear and loathing, I am certainly aware that there are plenty of people who do not feel the way I do. I am also aware that, logically, they are in the right. If death is certain ("Most things may never happen: this one will," Larkin observed dryly) and 'tis certain that it is certain, what then is the point of resistance? Perhaps none. Nevertheless, I do not believe that people accept death simply because it is certain. I think they come to death long before death comes to them, precisely because they have a predisposition or a longing for the annihilation of the self. And, yes, there are odd moments when even I have a glimmering of why someone might be half in love with easeful death: It is flawless and forever, before and beyond everything one might imagine. Edward Thomas's "Rain" puts it better than I can:

> Like me who have no love which this wild rain
> Has not dissolved except the love of death,
> If love it be toward what is perfect and
> Cannot, the tempest tells me, disappoint.

Perhaps for certain people it might well be something approaching love, if love means wanting to get as close as one can to something or, in this case, to Nothing.

The awful thing is that Hazlitt is probably right. Those who desperately cling to life do not embrace it, and the tighter one clings the more difficult it is to let go; while those who love life with a passionate but realistic view of its limitations are best reconciled to leaving it behind. How am I supposed to handle this? Epicurus tells me that death is nothing to me and shouldn't concern me, since nothing and I will never co-exist. Seneca advises me to "rehearse death" and keep it close, so that its universal nature will become apparent. Shakespeare's Julius Caesar finds it is "most strange that man must fear; seeing that death, a necessary end, will come when it will come." Jonathan Swift assures me that "It is impossible that anything so natural, so necessary, and so universal as death, should ever have been designed by providence as an evil to mankind." A Zen koan teaches that "While living / Be a dead man / Be thoroughly dead— / And behave as you like / And all's well." Tibetan Buddhism tells me not to think of life and death in opposition to one another. And Hazlitt tells me to stop thinking about it entirely.

Perhaps I will when I'm dead. In the meantime, I acknowledge the necessity of dying. We all have to go sometime, we all have this duty to perform or else "all" would become far too many and messy. Nevertheless, I prefer not to die. But what if everyone felt this way, what if everyone decided to live forever? To which I reply, borrowing from Joseph Heller's Assyrian airman: "Then I'd be a damned fool to feel any other way, wouldn't I?" So do I really want to be immortal? I think I do, actually—providing that I don't become like one of Swift's dementia-ridden Struldbruggs or Tennyson's aged and sickly Tithonus ("Me only cruel immortality consumes"). At the very least, I want to have the choice.

And whoever encourages me to see the upside only nudges me in the opposite direction. Sure, mortality has its claims, Adam Phillips admits, but that by itself is not a bad thing. Go back to Freud and Darwin and you may wonder whether "ageing, accident, illness and death [are] not alien but integral to our sense of ourselves . . . whether loss is still the right word." Well, I am here to tell you that it is still the right word. We are born to lose: to lose our innocence, our youth, our agility, and our health. If we live long enough, we lose our parents, our friends, our spouses; we may even lose our children; we all lose one another and then we lose ourselves. Life is the gradual loss of everything, including loss.

Therefore, I choose to regard life as a struggle whose stakes are so high that defeat is unimaginable: Vanquished, I vanish. And this—this seems a terrible waste of time. All the work that went into making me undeniably Me—for what? There is something inefficient about building a person and then having the person die. If you think of the ego as one of those elaborate frigates ensconced in a bottle and the effort it took to construct and glue sails, masts, rigging, spars, and halyards, why then it's a crying shame when that bottle falls off the mantel and shatters, and the ship breaks up and splinters beyond repair.

Unhealthy, unenviable, and ridiculous as this outlook undoubtedly is, it's my own. Sensible people will cluck and remonstrate. Kindly people will urge me to buck up. But, you know, I don't want advice or comfort. I want only to maintain the sense of outrage necessary to rail at what I cannot change. Adam Phillips and his ilk notwithstanding, I see death as the bully in the schoolyard waiting to knock my block off. And when he does, I hope to get in a few good licks and curse him and the pale horse he rode in on. That "special way of being afraid" that Larkin knew all too well, I do, too: "No trick dispels." One day the bully *will* find me, and when that day comes, I plan to remember that "fear oppresses strength" and "fearing dying pays death servile breath." I'll be afraid all right, but anger brushes fear aside, and if I'm lucky I shall meet death clear-eyed and pissed off, and I'll put up such a struggle that next time he'll think twice about taking me.

[2001]

6

Why Smart People Believe in God

L ately, I have been mulling over my relationship with God. Well, not mine exactly, but other people's. And, to be honest, I wouldn't be doing any mulling at all if these were not subtitled films–PBS–*New York Review of Books* people (they may not have read Darwin, but they've read Stephen Jay Gould on Darwin); people who routinely vote the liberal or progressive ticket, scoff at evangelical preachers, cast an ironic eye on conceptual art, and, all the same, can look me in the eye and say, "I am not alone." And when they do, I wonder what trick of temperament allows them such certainty and keeps me outside this particular existential loop. It's a pretty futile business, of course, talking about religion, especially if it is someone else's. The best remark (and wisest course of action) on the subject that I know was rendered by H. L. Mencken: "We must respect the other fellow's religion, but only in the sense and to the extent that we respect his theory that his wife is beautiful and his children smart."

It's easy enough to understand why people want to believe, but to actually believe with one's whole heart and mind in divine grace, that to me is a true miracle. And now that I am entering my middle age, it seems natural, to tweak a phrase, to sit upon the ground and tell sad stories of the death of gods. Please don't be misled: I may have my share of metaphysical pathos, but it's not as if the eternal silence of infinite spaces troubles me overmuch. What's agitating me is religion envy, an unjustifiable resentment of intelligent and skeptical people—I almost said "people who ought to know better"—who swim effortlessly toward the sanctity of dry land, while others, like myself, spiritually adrift, seem unable to strike out for shore. I don't mind admitting that I am flummoxed by their groundedness, their conviction, their serenity.

You can read an awful lot of books on the subject of God, from the simple-minded tracts that posit His existence on the basis of our existence to the searching arguments put forward by learned theologians (who seem to be mostly Swiss or German: Barth, Buber, Bultmann, Tillich, Niebuhr, Küng), for whom God is not just a reflex when death comes tapping. Whatever else propels such books, there is a common desire to view revealed religion organically, as part of the human condition. Protestant, Catholic, or Jewish, the authors are intent on erasing the line between earthly existence and divinity, between history and eschatology. Making the miraculous plausible takes various forms: some pay out intellectual dividends; others do not. At one extreme, there are apologists who advocate strict adherence to Scripture because Scripture demands such obedience; at the other extreme, philosophers offer proofs of God's existence that often spiral into a Hegelian rigmarole of God as thought or pure essence in the process of becoming known-in-and-for-us as Absolute Spirit. There are also literary commentators like the odious Hilaire Belloc and the somewhat less anti-Semitic G. K. Chesterton, who profess their veneration for Christ and their dislike of those outside of Christ. And in our own day, such theologically minded novelists as

A. N. Wilson and Reynolds Price continue to bring us the good news without ceding too much intellectual ground.

The millennium is certainly good news for the religious publishing industry. Last year there were 2,657 titles of a general religious nature, a few of which migrated from Evangelical Christian bookstores to the mass-market chains. Most weeks you can find one or two books dealing with God on the *New York Times* Paperback Best Sellers list (apocalyptic warnings and personal accounts of salvation are the staple here), and even the vaunted *Times* hardcover list featured, for nearly two years, *Conversations with God: Book 1* by Neale Donald Walsch. This is a country where God sells, and where an ill-considered remark by a public figure— such as Minnesota governor Jesse Ventura's characterization of organized religion as "a crutch for the weak-minded"—still merits headlines. Opiate of the masses religion may be, but it certainly doesn't dull our senses to aspersions cast its way.

One doesn't, of course, come to God through books (the Bible is confirmation of treasure found, not the quest for it), but through the realization that a higher power is responsible for individual existence, that one's life has no ultimate meaning unless it is enfolded within that power. Slowly forming epiphanies are just as valid as the vocal, blinding light that turned Saul into Paul. Yes, you can avoid Him your whole life, but that doesn't mean that the impulse to believe has been quieted. But belief in what?

> Some say that we shall never know and that to the gods we are
> like the flies that the boys kill on a summer day, and some say,
> on the contrary, that the very sparrows do not lose a feather
> that has not been brushed away by the finger of God.

Here, tenderly put, in Thornton Wilder's *Bridge of San Luis Rey* (with a nod to *King Lear*), is the crux of the matter: Either God is the conscientious foreman overseeing our individual tasks, or He (in the form of pluralistic gods) is the pantheistic creator who quits the premises once we've clocked in. If God is indeed a God who pokes His finger into the muck of human experience (so He's responsible for the Mets losing the pennant this year!) then such a God I presume to scan. Any deity that enters into relations with such imperfect creatures as ourselves automatically grants us access. The God of tests and demands, the sacrificing-of-your-only-son, vengeance-is-mine deity who behaves like a spoiled king when his subjects get antsy or rebellious is a God I can take issue with.

If, on the other hand, God is an entity *pace* Nicholas of Cusa, whose circumference is nowhere and whose center is everywhere, whose divine essence is infinite, whose swirling galaxies, black holes, and burning gaseous matter are constantly being replenished, and whose very nature is indistinguishable from the cosmic pinball machine that we see only a corner of (He, being, of course, both game and sole player), then the question properly becomes: Why would this boundless, never-ending, self-perpetuating, worlds-upon-worlds God pay attention to *us*? No way that this ineffable, overarching force would make a covenant with Abraham, reveal Itself to Moses, visit Mary, or require our breathless adoration. Herein lies the implicit heresy in Giordano Bruno's likening of God to an infinite geometry, a view of the universe that, along with other semi-mystical persuasions, led to his auto-da-fé in 1600.

There is, of course, no contradiction in a God of infinite spaces and of a localized region in space. If He's everywhere, then He's also got to be right here. Logically, this is correct; emotionally, though, it doesn't compute. To say it again: Why would the God whose reach exceeds our grasp by billions of light years give any thought to the likes of us? All of human history is not the width of a fraction of a hair compared to the history of the universe. But who can conceive it? Who would want to? Most of us, in fact, don't. For all the talk of His grandeur, the true believer tends to see God as a stern but loving paterfamilias, ready to lend a helping hand or smite His children with same should they merit it. Fundamentalists of every stripe are like the provincial inhabitants of small villages in out-of-the-way places. They spend their lives in a Kentucky hollow or Tuscan hill town, where the greater world— apart from the occasional overhead plane or TV show—makes few inroads. They have their work, their families, their friends, and when they find themselves in trouble, they turn to the local magistrate. If it's a spiritual problem, there is always Scripture. To such people, whose devotion to Pat Robertson, the Pope, the Rebbe, or the Ayatollah is absolute, God is essentially the Mayor of the planet. And though I'm tempted to write off everyone who believes in the literal truth of the Old and New Testaments, the Koran, and the Book of Mormon, simply because these were books written and translated by mortals, the fact that religious texts are the handiwork of fallible men and women does not by itself disprove the existence of God.

This God, the God of the book—there's no other way of saying it—is a stunted God, who apparently has nothing better to do than hang around our teeny section of the galaxy and amuse Himself at our expense by creating or allowing situations that, as the devout like to say, confound the wise. (Ask yourself: Why would God wish to confound the wise?) You may not be bothered by a hands-on God who lets loose with massacres and disease, but I am. You may argue that the often terrible and meaningless events inflicted on human beings, usually by other human beings, are part of His mysterious ways, but I say that the local authorities should be held accountable. The God of colon and cervical cancer, multiple sclerosis, Alzheimer's disease, puss, phlegm, shit, chancre sores, still birth and crib death, poverty, famine, war, pestilence, race hatred, paralysis, constipation and incontinence, child molestation, floods, earthquakes and accidents, rape, mutilation, botched medical procedures, death marches, Zyklon-B, despair, and suicide is a God who has a lot to answer for. He's got the whole world in His hands, and they're covered with blood.

True, He is also the God of natural wonders, of cloudless climes and starry skies, perhaps even of the occasional miracle, but if you're going to weigh the good against the bad, the bad wins hands down. The celestial bureaucrat who allows bad things to happen is, of course, the God of Job; and to pray to this God is, to my way of thinking, an act both futile and demeaning. It's like believing that the stingy and mean-spirited boss will give you a bonus for sucking up. The true believer, however, takes all this in stride and, should perplexity or doubt creep in, barely misses a step. There is, after all, an explanation. Sixteen centuries ago, the existence of both God and evil in the world was reconciled by Augustine of Hippo, who, in acknowledging both, maintained that: (1) since God cannot be evil, the source of evil in the world lies within us; (2) this evil sprang from Adam's misuse of his free will, which led him to sin, a sin that is passed on by his descendants; (3) the same agency that contrives to sin is also what makes faith so powerful, since without free will (and the capacity to disavow Him), our devotion to Him would have no meaning. Thus God makes it difficult to love Him, because without such difficulty our love would be no more than the love a puppy feels for its master. Life then becomes a measure of our desire to reach Him, to prove ourselves worthy of Him.

It is this God as Mayor who also figures in Pascal's famous wager in the *Pensées:* If God does not exist, but you conduct yourself as if He does, then all you stand to lose is a mere sixty years or so of having led a decent existence. Now weigh this behavior against leading a disreputable life for sixty years and the possibility that He exists: The God-fearing life will be rewarded for all eternity, whereas the sinful life will be punished for all eternity. Given the risk, it makes sense to play it safe. And that is just what I don't like about this God. If He is small enough to feel

slighted by my disbelief in His existence or annoyed by my un-
willingness to play by His rules, and sends me to Hell, then to Hell
with Him. If such a God exists, why would I want to spend
eternity with the likes of Him? And if He exists, I hope I shall have
the courage to tell Him off. Just because I may end up acknowledging Him doesn't mean I have to approve of Him. Call this—with
apologies to Jonathan Edwards—my "God in the Hands of an
Angry Sinner" sermon.

As for the notion of original sin itself, don't get me started.
That such a strange, distasteful, self-flagellating view of human life
has any currency at all is enough to make a reasonable person want
to move to a land where Christianity is prohibited. I don't mean to
make light of the problem of evil, but the truth is, evil is a Christian
rather than a philosophical preoccupation. Without faith, the existence of evil isn't a theological problem at all; it's simply a fact that
skews the idea of an absolute or perfect universe, a notion that
Plato and the Neo-Platonists were rather keen on. And with or
without the Judeo-Christian God, isn't it reasonable to think of
creation as perfect rather than imperfect, in which case how does
the noticeably bad or trivial fit into the picture?

Equating God with the world while acknowledging the world's
imperfections clearly required theological spin doctors of a high
order. Happily for the Church, such a man came along in 1225, and
for sheer intellectual brazenness he is hard to beat. St. Thomas
Aquinas practically dares us not to believe. Things seem bad? Well,
the worse they seem, the better it all is. Starting from the premise of
God's limitless nature and unceasing activity, Aquinas deduces that
"the perfection of the universe is attained essentially in proportion
to the diversity of natures in it." Sounds kind of dry, but consider
the implications: "A universe in which there was no evil would not
be so good as the actual universe." Aquinas is also capable of
arguing that simply because an angel is better than a stone does not
mean that two angels are necessarily better than one angel and one

stone. In other words, things are as they should be, or they wouldn't be as they are.

W hat, I can imagine someone asking, does any of this have to do with faith? Faith isn't about explaining logical implausibilities, it's about accepting a narrative that accounts for creation and that molds itself into a person's moral and emotional raison d'être. Belief in God is no more subject to doubt than belief in existence itself. But here, too, lies a problem, since we cannot speak of God without endowing Him with human attributes, including the most fundamental attribute of all: existence. Six hundred years before the Council of Nicaea, in 325, officially wrestled with the problem of Christ's divine essence in light of his human existence, Aristotle surmised that existence can never belong to the essence of a thing. This concept, alien, I think, to many believers, was taken up by the twentieth-century theologian Paul Tillich, who followed it to its natural end: "If you start with the question of whether God does or does not exist, you can never reach Him; and if you assert that He does exist, you can reach Him even less than if you assert that He does not exist." Obviously, for purposes of explication, it's necessary to talk about Him in such terms and, less obviously, this is where President Clinton's hedging about the most basic verb in our language becomes relevant: If God cannot take a predicate, then His existence may, in fact, depend on what your definition of "is" is.

Arguments for His existence, however, can never be anything more than analogical speculations that the world requires a Being greater than it in order for the world to exist. Were such a Being to exist, the argument continues, the universe would conform to an elegantly laid-out plan, a simple and beautifully realized system of natural checks and balances that eventually will become apparent to scientists. Putting aside for the moment the question of whether elegance itself is absolute proof of God's existence, it seems to me that the peerless God who may or may not preside over this splendid but frameless masterpiece, who is both the process of creation and the creator of the process, is (once again) at odds with the Lord our God, who's made such a mess of things. This split in thinking about God goes back to the first two centuries A.D., when a group of loosely connected Gnostic philosophers proposed that the God of the book was actually a Demi-urge, who was Himself created by the True God, of whom the Demi-urge is totally unaware. In effect, the God to whom we pray is a stand-in, the unwitting buffer for the One of whom we cannot speak.

I doubt that many people try to reconcile these two visions of God: the amorphous unknowable Being and our resident *genius loci*. People drawn to God, but not to a specific faith, usually resolve the issue by opting in favor of the former and then trying to find links that bring Him closer to home or that make His unavailability more tenable. But the more ineffable the God, the fewer the links. If, for example, God is pure essence that does not conceive Itself to be, since It always was and always must be, then time cannot be a condition of Its existence, and we, as temporal beings, shouldn't worry our heads about It or it. But we do, and to what avail? Any argument you muster against the plausibility of His existence, any points you make about the contradictions inherent in a God both deistic and revelatory, simply won't cut ice with true believers. "The Son of God has died; this is credible because it is absurd," Tertullian wrote. "Buried, He has risen again; this is certain because it is impossible." No logic from him; no argument from me.

Why do I mention all these obstacles to belief? Not because these are hurdles the nonbeliever cannot surmount, but because they are hurdles the intellectually inclined believer *must* surmount.

St. Ignatius Loyola says somewhere that the sacrifice most welcomed by God is the sacrifice of our intellect. I wonder. Is the
impulse to find God automatic grounds for dismissal of the intellect? Is the intellectual high ground reserved for the atheist alone?
One of the reasons—perhaps the main reason—the secular thinker
has problems with the pious is that he confuses the demarcation
between atheism and belief with the feelings that the respective
camps have for one another. Whereas the secular humanist considers it part of his job description to repudiate the tenants of
religion, the thoughtful believer finds no actual disharmony between humanism and religion; those who believe do not necessarily believe *in opposition* to those who do not believe.

Although it would be foolhardy to generalize about the pres-
ence and intensity of belief in the general population, it might be
fair to say that among intellectuals there seems to be less soul-
searching these days than in the century that gave birth to Darwin,
Marx, and Nietzsche. Those of us disinclined to believe have
grown accustomed to His absence and pay but a small price for
our uncertainty or feelings of abandonment as compared with
writers such as Dostoevsky and Camus, who either wrestled with
their doubts or expressed their dismay at the decision they felt
bound to make. Which of our writers or philosophers today are
tortured by the prospect of having to make a choice?

The problem of belief, which had once seemed part of the
intellectual community's charter, could still be discerned as late as
1950, when Paul Tillich, in "Religion and the Intellectuals," felt
justified in characterizing the response to the question of God as
inevitably "negative-religious" or "positive-religious." The former,
characterized by despair over the human predicament, accepts this
despair and endeavors "heroically" through art or philosophy "to
create a meaning of the meaningless." The positive-religious response, reacting to the same predicament, transcends it by "radically transforming it into a question to which religion gives the

answer," not by the surrender of one's intellectual autonomy to biblical authorities (which is also a sign of despair), but by finding a religious answer "which does not destroy reason but points to the depth of reason; which does not teach the supernatural, but points to the mystery in the ground of the natural, which denies that God is a being . . . [which] resists the distortion of symbols into statements of knowledge which necessarily conflict with scientific knowledge." The positive-religious approach, it would seem, can, unlike the negative-religious, both comprehend man's despair *and* express the "answers to the questions implied in man's existence and existence generally."

I think not. The human predicament, about which Tillich has no illusions, is simply not the same for those who believe and those who do not. However diligently the religious intellectual adumbrates a universe in which God necessarily resides, that universe (whatever the level of despair) is not the one in which the nonbeliever resides. The dichotomy is as simple as it is inescapable: For the believer, faith and truth are one word; for the nonbeliever, faith must be borne out by truth. There are, needless to say, any number of intellectuals, as opposed to professional theologians, who have willingly accepted religious dogma of one kind or another. Few, however, have articulated such faith with the forceful cogency of T. S. Eliot. Although Eliot wrote relatively little about his confirmation in the Church of England, he not only took it seriously, but took exception to the idea that humanism, being rational, stands apart from religion: "Most people suppose that some people, because they enjoy the luxury of Christian sentiments and the excitement of Christian ritual, swallow or pretend to swallow incredible dogma. For some the process is exactly opposite. Rational assent may arrive late, intellectual conviction may come slowly, but they come inevitably without violence to honesty and nature."

And they come because, sooner or later, we recognize that for

a system of morals to be absolute, it must have a religious foundation—otherwise such a system is, by default, relativistic, based on
cultural (that is, temporal) sets of values. Perfectly willing to accept
the humanist's position that "the essential reality of experience is
ethical," Eliot is also quick to point out that the statement cannot
have the same meaning for the religious person and the person
who disavows religion. Just so there's no mistaking what *he* means,
Eliot asserts: "Either everything in man can be traced as a development from below, or something must come from above. There is
no avoiding that dilemma: You must be either a naturalist or a
supernaturalist."

You could do worse than read Pascal's *Pensées* to understand
why smart people believe in God. The wager notwithstanding, the *Pensées* strikes me as the most ardent and intelligent study
of man's relationship to God that any philosopher has undertaken.
Rereading Pascal after nearly twenty-five years, I'm prepared to
admit that his anxiety is real, that his fear and loathing of annihilation make him as modern as any gloomy Sartre-spouting Sixties
existentialist. I think Pascal really does feel the pull of Nothingness, but as a mathematician and scientist he also believes that
man's dignity is bound up with the power of thought. And thinking forces him to admit that "the end of things and their beginning" are hopelessly hidden from him, and that he's "equally
incapable of seeing the Nothing from which he was made, and the
Infinite in which he is swallowed up."

But Pascal's skepticism, if not his melancholy, is ultimately a
pose. His despair over the disorder and futility of life never
brushes a molecule off God's sleeve. He's a true believer in every
one of the 923 fragments, and the paradoxical two-step he per-
forms in order to convince himself that the heart has reasons which

reason does not know (number 277) recalls Nicholas of Cusa's observation that: "There is no proportionality between the finite and the infinite." Being finite, Pascal cannot draw any conclusions about the infinite, so the possibility of God's existence is just as incomprehensible as the possibility of His non-existence. Yet the world must be accounted for; and if the heart truly knows that God made the world, then reason itself is redeemed by Christ. This affirmation of the heart's wisdom is not, Eliot claims, a simplistic defense of intuition over intellect, or heart over head, but a short-hand for the complicated struggle that culminates in belief, a way of talking about faith as the fusion of feeling and thinking in which "the whole personality is involved."

Eliot reads Pascal the way Pascal reads the world: he takes him on faith. The truth is, Eliot's commentary, far from being unimpeachable, only bears out William James's dissection of the connective tissue between personality and philosophy. For James, the philosopher is always the whole man, who "like every human being of the slightest mental originality . . . is particularly sensitive to evidence that bears in some one direction." For what it's worth, I believe this. I believe that we enter this world as interested parties rushing to a crime scene; we arrive with built-in biases and see what we're inclined to see. So, frankly, I'm amazed that intellectuals are convinced of the Mayor's existence, but I accept their faith, as well as their condescension toward people like myself. C. S. Lewis once compared the amiable agnostic's talk of man's search for God to that of a mouse's search for the cat. I like that, but not the idea that the cat is necessarily in the house. Although I am not, as you have probably noticed, an *amiable* agnostic, nonetheless I'd like to believe; I'd like to experience the peace felt by the *religieuse*. Even the die-hard atheist must feel a certain pause when pondering the detailed fabric of the universe or witnessing the birth of a child. And when loved ones pass on, how can we not secretly hope that a higher power will look after them, and help us to meet up again?

And, lest we forget, there remains that tetchy problem of creation. Something happened, and here we are. And for something to have happened, there had to have been something at the beginning, because from nothing, nothing can come. This feels right, and yet one may also feel that from the God of the Bible this universe could not have come. Still, it's awfully tempting to accept the Thomistic portrait of God as prime mover, first cause, and pure act—otherwise, what we're left with is an infinite regress in which we go back in time, and back, and end up only going back some more. How can we make sense of existence? Whence did it all begin?

I suspect that Christianity offers the best occasion for an intense feel-good religious experience. Christianity, after all, has the enviable fillip of a God willing to die for our sins so that we might enter heaven. To believe that God loves you so much is surely cause to return that love. This phenomenon of loving, or coming to, God is so widely attested that one would have to be somewhat perverse to ignore it. To see the delight on the faces of those who sing His praises, to hear the Mass at Christmas, to attend evensong is to feel more than anything else that one has been left out of the secret. It is also to understand that the devout do not simply believe in God, they *experience* God, and only a fool would prefer the pride of the cynic to such knowledge.

The wise, in fact, are not confounded. I take it for granted that clever, intellectually sophisticated people experience God as deeply as do ecstatic snake-handling Pentecostals. Faith is a personal matter, of course, but for the educated believer it may be something more. When a scientist, engineer, artist, or mathematician solves a particularly knotty problem, the resultant exhilaration is more than an egotistical reaction to having beaten the competition or the odds. It derives from discovering a pattern, from finding the missing piece that suddenly makes the work right, and there is something immensely satisfying in this. The same elation undoubtedly overcomes the rational skeptic when the truth hits home, when suddenly everything makes sense. The contradictions in the Bible, the lack of hard evidence, the existence of accident and evil no longer signify, because a world without God is even more absurd than a world with Him. Faith is where all syllogisms fail; it is overwhelming, deep, wonderful, and real—and it makes sense. The wise who have found God don't wish to understand creation in order to believe, they believe in order to understand. And I expect that it must feel pretty damn good. I expect that God gets certain people high in the same way that Nature or the Sublime used to get Wordsworth and Coleridge high.

Still, you have to allow others the right of refusal; some can't or won't inhale transcendence. The biblical God is out of the question, not because of intellectual scruples, but because of a temperamental predilection to go it alone, if He is the alternative. "The only excuse for [this] God," Stendhal remarked, "is that He does not exist." What remains? Perhaps the possibility one day of finding that the coalescing, excoriating infinite geometry that has neither beginning nor ending will actually make sense to me. The thundering irony here is that although this is a God I could believe in, He's not One who's going to do me much good. Nonetheless, it is this God that those of us who don't believe, but would like to, must seek. And how do we go about looking for Him? "It is not when I am going to meet him, but when I am just turning away and leaving him alone," Thoreau wrote, "that I discover that God is." Well, Mister, I am turning away . . . turning . . . turning. Who shall catch me before I'm gone?

[2001]

7

Taste, Too, Is an Art

J ohn Updike and I do not see eye to eye. Reviewing the Andy
Warhol retrospective at the Museum of Modern Art for the
New Republic (March 27, 1989), Updike took the occasion to
pronounce Warhol a "considerable philosopher." Relying on
The Philosophy of Andy Warhol for his text, Updike cites:
"Some critic called me the Nothingness Himself and that didn't
help my sense of existence any. Then I realized that existence itself
is nothing and I felt better." Hmm. If this observation qualifies as
considerable philosophy, surely any number of high school students have achieved equal philosophical sophistication.

But Updike is an intelligent man and must have reason to
admire Warhol. Indeed, he goes so far as to say that some of
Warhol's remarks "have the penetrating desolation we associate
with maximists like La Rochefoucauld and Chamfort." What is the
evidence for this claim? According to Updike, it's this: "I think
that just being alive is so much work at something you don't always
want to do. Being born is like being kidnapped. And then sold
into slavery." Adds Updike: "The equation of being born with
being kidnapped takes one's breath away." There is, I suppose,

something to be said for the conceit that life is snatched from the
maw of Nothingness, in which case death is a ransom of sorts, but
one's breathing is hardly disturbed by the disclosure. As for com-
paring these rather sophomoric observations with those by La
Rochefoucauld or Chamfort, one may be permitted to disagree.
And yet Updike is an intelligent man, whose opinion should count
for something.

Intelligence, clearly, is no guarantor of compatible philosophical, aesthetic, or moral outlooks among people. Intelligent people
disagree all the time about books, movies, music, humor, and
other people. And when otherwise intelligent, well-meaning people find value in ideas and things that leave us cold, we're puzzled,
perhaps we're bothered, certainly we're disappointed. But as intelligent, well-meaning people, we accept their views because—well,
because we prize the idea of individuality, because we sense that
heterogeneity is part of the human condition and should not be
tampered with or repressed.

In a word—and that word is spelled t-a-s-t-e—we surrender;
we allow that other people have a right to their opinions and that
no one opinion should cancel out another. The cant is now part of
the language: One man's meat is another man's poison; different
strokes for different folks; *chacun à son goût*. Taste has become the
ultimate shrug in the face of diversity, a catchword that says my
response to a poem or flavor of ice cream is no more and no less
valid than yours.

Democratic, to be sure, but does the fact that everyone has an
equal right to an opinion mean that all opinions are equal? The
way some people decorate their homes or themselves, or choose
what they eat and drink, may demonstrate only that they know no
better. To prefer Gallo to Chambertin means simply that one's
taste buds are dead to the grape. Tastes may be equal in one sense,
but wines are not. For that matter, one can admire another per-

son's work while acknowledging that one would do things differently. It may not be fashionable to say so, but some people have taste in paintings where others do not; some palates are able to taste what other palates cannot, and certain books will remain unappreciated until taste is shaped and enhanced by study and familiarity—a view of things, it should be said, that caused hardly a ripple of consternation for the greater part of human history.

For centuries, taste was an accredited part of the intellectual order. Individual tastes may have differed, but the *idea* of taste, the application of taste, whether in the making or in the appreciation of various artifacts, brooked no dispute. Strict laws of decorum governed painting and verse, as well as behavior, and one acquired an appreciation of art much as one acquired, pedigree permitting, skill at arms. The rabble could no more demonstrate proper taste than the correct use of a rapier—an outlook that was, needless to say, grounded in the aristocracy's wish to define itself at the expense of peasants and shopkeepers.

All the same, it was not a demotic movement that sought to do away with such high-minded conduct where art and literature were concerned. The first stirring of discontent with sovereign taste arose during the Quarrel between the Ancients and the Moderns in the first half of the seventeenth century. Hesitantly, and then more forcefully, writers and painters began to question the degree of observance owed to the rules of decorum (which even the ancient writers were retroactively held to). For many reasons, not least of which was the embryonic belief in Progress, the Moderns gradually prevailed. And with their victory, which reflected the victory of inductive, observational methods over the Scholastic tendency to "save appearances," the rules of decorum, or *les bienséances,* were rendered harmless. By the time the category of aesthetics was created in the mid-eighteenth century, the idea of taste (and tastes) was ready to change.

Retaining its original meaning as a response to physical stimuli, the word "taste" soon began to be identified with the sympathetic effects produced by art. But without guidelines and rules to
define it, taste became a rather thorny issue. To some writers, it
suggested only the unverifiable opinions of interested parties. To
others, it represented nothing less than the mental faculty of forming judgments, whose potential was such that it could, in the
words of Walter Jackson Bate, be "augmented and directed by
experience and learning, and which in time may acquire an almost
intuitional sagacity in its objective insight."

To a point, the problem of taste reflected the problem of all
modern philosophy, which might be summed up by the question:
How do we logically determine the cognitive relations between
thought and experience, so that sense-impressions, which may be
unreliable, can still be considered objectively valid? Though never
a philosophical issue on the order of ethics, causality, or the Will,
the question of taste managed to engage such philosophers and
philosophical critics as Kant, Schiller, Joseph Addison, James Beattie, Alexander Gerard, and Dugald Stewart. A glance at any bibliography of works devoted to eighteenth-century aesthetics reveals a
dozen or so "Essays," "Observations," and "Some Remarks" on
the subject of taste. In one such influential work, *Discourses Delivered to the Students of the Royal Academy* (1769–90), Sir Joshua
Reynolds lifts taste to unprecedented heights. Taste, Reynolds argues, while it may signify the emotional response occasioned by
things, is, in fact, the ability to distinguish between opinions and
prejudices—that is, "truth upon sufferance, or truth by courtesy"—
and those truths that please because they approach the ideal found
in nature.

Reynolds, being a man of his time, could not divest himself of
the classicist belief in an immutable reality; nonetheless, his definition of truth was not so strict that he could not apply it to the

imaginative and evolving works produced in the name of art, whose nature may be gleaned by study and familiarity, the better to determine which of them transcend individual opinions and social customs. Accordingly, a certain philosophical disposition was necessary to receive art's true impressions, and genuine taste was intrinsic to this receptivity. To quote W. Jackson Bate again: "Taste is 'good' or 'bad' in proportion to its capacity to gauge the extent and quality of this truth; it is, in short, the 'power of distinguishing right from wrong' in the arts." What Reynolds makes plain is that taste arrives with learning and constitutes nothing less than "the real labour of thinking."

Nonetheless, such "labour" was not for everyone, and whatever cultural footing "taste" may have attained toward the end of the eighteenth century, it was relatively short-lived. Although Reynolds had hoped taste would become a synonym for educated judgment, the word could not hold up under the weight of common usage; its frequent appearance in conversation and print to indicate individual likes and dislikes eventually clouded its association with rational thought; and a generation after Reynolds's *Discourses*, taste's philosophical connotations had all but disappeared. Only sporadically would they resurface.

O ddly enough, one such attempt at resurrection appears in Susan Sontag's "*Notes on 'Camp*,'" published in 1964 at a time when all tastes seemed licensed. "To patronize the faculty of taste," writes Sontag, "is to patronize oneself. For taste governs every free—as opposed to rote—human response. Nothing is more decisive. There is taste in people, visual taste, taste in emotion— and there is taste in acts, taste in morality. Intelligence, as well, is really a kind of taste: taste in ideas." Thus, to apologize for one's own tastes or to excuse another's taste is to slight one's ability to

make informed judgments, for ultimately what leads us to prefer
Proust over Sidney Sheldon is not *chacun à son goût* but rather
"the real labour of thinking." To prefer is to think.

Yet we prefer to think that "preference" itself hardly constitutes a subject for intellectual debate. Indeed, when the word
"taste" appears in any discussion concerning human intercourse,
an anachronistic whiff of Toryism seems to hover in the air. To
accuse someone of a lack of taste is to hint at all sorts of shortcom-
ings ranging from a natural boorishness to a deprived upbringing,
all of which in the end shout "class!" Consequently, as Rochelle
Gurstein notes in *The Repeal of Reticence,* a book that outlines
America's struggles over free speech and obscenity, "taste has no
public resonance at all; rather, it has been drastically reduced to
mean little more than individual whim or consumer preference. In
consequence, judgments about which things should appear in
public, speculation about the common good, as well as delibera-
tion about moral and aesthetic matters, have increasingly been
relegated to the obscurity of the private realm, leaving everyone to
his or her own devices."

Given the current intellectual and political climate, this is a
rather brave regret to voice. Imagine: the exercise of taste being
identified with the common good, as if useful and intelligent approaches to life were actually a function of taste. Of course, when
speaking about the common good, we assume that men and
women, if properly apprised of the human situation, will agree as
to what is good and bad, significant and trivial, right and wrong.
This is what Hazlitt meant when he observed that "it does not
follow, because there is no dogmatic or bigoted standard of
taste . . . that there is no standard of taste whatsoever. . . . In a
word, fine taste consists in sympathy, not in antipathy." It is pretty
to think so, but people's understanding of things are bound to be
different, and sympathies will clash.

Still, the idea of a common sympathy make sense if only because it implies comprehension; it's hard to sympathize, after all, with what one doesn't understand. And if we agree that the mind is molded by the character of what it contemplates, then surely those who make a point of contemplating the arts are its most astute critics. Unfortunately, experience does not always bear this out; and the reason lies in experience itself. If knowledge *pace* Kant begins with experience, then each person's ideas derive, at least in part, from the personal and private events that affected him; and therefore every philosophical system must issue from a subjective viewpoint or, if you will, taste. (It was Kant, not incidentally, who wished to attribute to taste both a subjective and objective aspect, by which one might make "the transition . . . from the charm of sense to habitual moral interest.")

As with artists and writers, philosophers have a personal stake in their work; first impressions, childhood traumas, adolescent neuroses, and personal tics also help form the philosopher's angle of vision. Nietzsche, for one, saw no reason to shirk the fact: "Every great philosophy has so far been the self-confession of its originator, and a kind of unintentional, unawares *mémoires.*" For the most part, however, philosophers have escaped the psychoanalytic scrutiny routinely applied to artists. To my knowledge, which may be bibliographically incomplete, it was not until 1980, with the appearance of Ben-Ami Scharfstein's *The Philosophers*, that any real attempt was made to connect the personalities of the major philosophers with their thoughts. In fact, Scharfstein is convinced, though not wholly convincing on the score, that "philosophy is qualified at every point . . . by personal needs and idiosyncratic emotions."

One philosopher discussed by Scharfstein would undoubtedly agree—up to a point. To William James, the "philosopher" is always the whole man, in whom "intellect, will, taste, and passion co-operate just as they do in practical affairs." No philosophy could be formulated, James maintained, without the contribution of the personality, because the philosopher "like every human being of the slightest mental originality . . . *is peculiarly sensitive to evidence that bears in some one direction"* (my italics).

At first glance, this might seem an apologia for subjectivity and for granting equality among tastes. But, in point of fact, James's observation, while giving a cursory nod to subjectivity (what, in the end, is not subjective?) may actually justify the formulation of hierarchical judgments. Once we have conceded that individual minds exhibit patterns of thought no less distinctive than the epidermal crosshatching on one's fingertips, it follows that opinions must differ, but it does not follow that all opinions are equal. Indeed, what is surprising is that people born with different talents and different degrees of the same talent, with a predisposition for excelling at different things, ever manage to agree on anything.

Thus, we can argue that while knowledge of a particular subject has no bias, *what* we choose to know and *what* we regard as important to know are the expressions of a specific predilection. So when we say "there is no accounting for taste," what we really mean is that another temperament exists whose thoughts have their own reasons. Temperament defines us, and in doing so makes other temperaments hard to fathom. Thus, someone of my temperament (in which tastes play a large part) could no more have arrived at John Updike's estimation of Warhol's intellectual powers than he could have access to Updike's physiological chemistry, moods, or memories. And given our respective temperaments, Updike will never persuade me that I am wrong, and no doubt I'll have the same luck with him.

Can one hope, then, that men and women of similar temperament will have similar tastes, especially if they have similar backgrounds and educations? No. Nor should that be the goal, for taste is nothing if not deeply personal and resentful of common consensus. Perfect accord in matters of art is a rather somber and stupefying idea. It simply won't do if everyone likes what I like. After all, a Wildean willfulness to be misunderstood underscores one's tastes, adding a certain élan to one's appreciations. It's only proper, therefore, that one knowledgeable person finds Andy Warhol's aphorisms profound, while another, equally knowledgeable person, finds Warhol an intellectual bust. Taste gives every person the right to know better than the next. Saunter into any lecture hall, boardroom, hotel lobby, or bar, and you'll find people who have all the answers, or know where to look, or know whether one should bother looking in the first place.

B ut this is not the end of the story. What may appear to be an intellectual impasse also suggests how we may get around it. The fact that individual tastes make universal agreement a pipe dream in no way invalidates the fact that taste, being a kind of innate partiality toward certain ways of thinking and feeling, makes some people—when this partiality is broadened and refined by study and experience—more qualified to pronounce judgment on certain subjects than others. The melancholic temperament may not be necessary in order for poets and philosophers to achieve eminence, as medieval physicians once believed, but something— some combination of proteins and experience—does contribute to a person's gifts, as well as the inclination to develop these gifts. More to the point, taste, or the study of taste, should be encouraged in the attempt to comprehend what it is that makes man a sentient being.

There are those born to create art, and others who, by dint of inclination and training, are best qualified to judge their efforts. The serious critic may hesitate to state unequivocally what is or is not great art, but he or she can with a fair share of confidence decide whether a particular sonnet by John Donne is better than one by Oliver Goldsmith. Some poems *are* better than others. Some paintings *are* better than others, and the same applies to all artifacts. Why is this notion so difficult to accept when we have no moral or ideological qualms in allowing that some musicians play better than others? This seems necessary to say only because high culture at the present time is viewed by many educators as an enemy of the populace, and this in turn causes a great many more people to forget that art has always been the product of talent, skill, inspiration, and labor; and so, to a degree, has been the appreciation of art.

There is, it should be said, nothing rigorous or systematic about such appreciation. Indeed, taste itself, if nurtured properly, bears an element of humility before the mystery at the heart of creation, living or insensate. What sympathetic person—artist or critic—believes that a work of art is reducible to formulae, to predetermined commands and responses? Even the strictest of critics and the most assiduous of artists must finally step back and acknowledge the mystery in a poem, painting, or composition for which there is finally no adequate explanation, and which frees it from political agendas and narrowly defined moral constraints.

Not everyone is happy with this scenario. To attribute to art the value of elusiveness is distressing to the temperament that requires concrete proof of merit or distinction. Of what help is elusiveness as a category? By definition it cannot be defined, therefore it cannot be disputed. By contrast, it's easy enough to identify established standards and hierarchies, and to devise semiotic or political strategies to knock them over. Elusiveness, like the idea of quality, is thus said to fall under the heading of standards devised by a cultural elite.

Artists know better. "Play like you play," advised Count Basie. "Play like you *think* [his italics], and then you got it, if you're going to get it. And whatever you get, that's you, so that's your story." What *it* is, the Count does not say. But we know what he means.

"It" was what Louis Armstrong believed you could not understand, if you had to ask what "it" was. But Basie makes another, more explicit point, one that we don't ordinarily associate with music: "Play like you *think.*" But what does thinking have to do with playing the blues? Basie, of course, knows whereof he speaks. One cannot help but play (or write or dance or design) except as one thinks, because in whatever we do, we exhibit a taste in ideas, we manifest a temperament attuned to evidence that bears in some one direction.

The linking up of William James and Count Basie is not exactly one that shouts to be made (this may be its first and only instance), but it's a connection that highlights how two very different people, separated from each other by race, class, and date of birth, can arrive at a similar outlook. Despite their differences, each knew something the other knew, and such knowledge came about because both temperaments were sympathetic to the making of art.

In short, the idea of taste transcends individual tastes, just as human nature supersedes all deviations from what is regarded properly as human. If some of us are born to understand certain things better than other things, it is a matter neither for rejoicing nor for lamenting; it is simply a matter of temperament. So for those who are sensitive to cadence, color, and texture, to the turning of a phrase and the expression of a thought, to the elusive relations among these elements, art will always be made well or ill, always defined by the quality of its intelligence and workmanship. For such as these, art will never be beyond debate; it shall simply exist beyond reproach.

[1988]

8

The Rule of Temperament

I f you've ever wondered why people who resemble each other in age, coloring, education, and background can disagree vehemently about matters great and small, you'll derive no comfort from Oliver Wendell Holmes, Jr.'s assessment of man's unwavering bumptiousness: "Deep-seated preferences cannot be argued about; you cannot argue a man into liking a glass of beer—and therefore when differences are sufficiently far-reaching, we try to kill the other man rather than let him have his way. But that is perfectly consistent with admitting that, so far as appears, his grounds are just as good as ours." Argument about comestibles is small beer, but Holmes, if I read him correctly, is getting at something more complicated than what tickles the palate. He is speaking of differences in temperament, and temperament, as his near contemporary Joseph Conrad observed, "whether individual or collective, is not amenable to persuasion."

Like Holmes, Conrad was onto something. Not being a native speaker of English, he may have heard in the word "temperament" echoes of a vanished authority. For two millennia "temperament" had explained people to themselves by identifying the physiological underpinnings of behavior. Derived from Hippocrates, the theory of temperament postulated four cardinal humors in the blood—sanguine, phlegm, and yellow and black bile—which Galen later funneled into nine modes of behavior. Because people were different and reacted differently to the same stimuli, it seemed obvious to the Ancients that each humor had its own characterological function, and that as long as all four existed in the proper proportion, one could enjoy a healthy emotional existence.

That a person entered the world predisposed to deal with it in certain ways seemed as good an explanation as any for the vagaries of human behavior. Some people preferred winter to summer, vegetables to meat, women to men, science to poetry, sloth to activity—all this was simply nature at work; and when nature broke down, both mind and body were affected. When Descartes wished to distance himself from thinkers incapable of differentiating between the real and the unreal, he chastised those "whose cerebella are so troubled and clouded by the violent vapors of black bile that they mistake the false for the true."

Things might have gone on like this for a while longer had not William Harvey, in 1628, demonstrated the blood's proper circulation, thereby putting an end to the humoral theory and effectively stripping temperament of its medical credentials. No longer part of nature, temperament fell from intellectual grace (at a time, not coincidentally, when Descartes was doubting the evidence of his senses, and poets were first challenging the rule of taste). With temperament now divorced from physiology, our vocabulary lost a term that linked psychological character to a physical origin. People may have continued to exhibit sanguine, choleric, phlegmatic, and melancholic behaviors, but these behaviors no longer had concrete, attributable causes. "Temperament" now merely *signified* but did not *justify* a person's attitudes and preferences; and a person's moral, religious, or philosophical outlook no longer stemmed from an innate or natural propensity.

Such psychology as did exist ("faculty psychology" was the term covering medieval theories of the mind) ultimately gave way to a mechanistic philosophy that saw the world and the human body as machines operating under precise physical laws. As for human behavior, its mysteries eventually fell within the purview of nineteenth-century associative psychologists and of philosophers who grappled with the problem of the Will. Attempts to reconcile the Will with the still-powerful influence of absolutes made for interesting philosophy, but such philosophy, while adumbrating the workings of the mind, could not adequately deal with human behavior. It was not until the alienist theories of the late nineteenth century (from which Freud began his own work) that psychological behavior again became strongly linked to physiological makeup.

Fanciful as the humoral theory now appears, its canonical treatment of both mind and body is, to a large extent, once again accepted in the medical community. While an excess of black bile does not cause depression, depression can be treated with chemicals. Electrochemical activity in the left frontal lobe of the brain is an indicator of mental disposition: those with greater activity are— well, happier. Mood affects the body's chemistry, and chemistry affects mood. Of course, to attribute differences of opinion solely to chemistry begs the question, since opinions stemming from one's gene pool are not so much right or wrong as they are inevitable. But while it would be foolhardy to claim that a person's intellectual bent derives from a physiological condition, is it not equally wrong to regard intellectual opinion purely as the result of disinterested thought?

William James, for one, rejected disinterestedness out of hand: "It is almost incredible that men who are themselves working philosophers should pretend that any philosophy can be, or ever has been, constructed without the help of personal preference, belief, or divination." That is to say, something in the person of the philosopher is already predisposed to make of experience the idealistic, empirical, or rationalistic scheme that attempts to comprehend that experience. If that is the case, if individual temperaments naturally lean toward specific world views, then the none-too-comforting result is an intellectual cul-de-sac, a relativistic morass in which all opinions and tastes have equal dominion.

What hope then for universal agreement about anything? If one is speaking in terms of particular likes and dislikes, the answer is obvious. Temperament is tautology: I like as I am inclined to like, and what I like, you may not like, or like in your own fashion. Nor will it matter if you and I are intellectually on the same page. "Now, as I'm writing this in complete calm," Wittgenstein wrote to Bertrand Russell, "I can see perfectly well that your value judgments are just as good and just as deep-seated as mine in me, and that I have no right to catechize you. But I see equally clearly, now, that for that very reason there cannot be any real relation of friendship between us." Such rifts are perhaps inevitable when one is as touchy as Wittgenstein, yet even when scholars are more serene, detachment is difficult. Confronted with the same atomic notations of quantum mechanics, Niels Bohr and Einstein concluded from the evidence two very different probabilities, one opting for change, the other for order.

It is a great pity that temperament has lost its authority in the modern lexicon. Otherwise, we would be able to signify with one word that it is the *whole person* (body as well as mind) who prefers Jean Rhys to Virginia Woolf, or William Butler Yeats to William Carlos Williams. For the truth is, we are not the sum of our likes and dislikes; we are a sum (never finally totaled) that likes and dislikes, that chooses and rejects. Nothing seems more obvious than the rule of temperament, yet we remain loath to acknowledge it. It's as if we're embarrassed to admit that nature plays a role in our abilities, talents, and preferences. But clearly when two people of similar backgrounds, interests, and intellectual attainment interpret the same evidence differently, something is at work besides intelligence.

To return in roundabout fashion to Conrad: "If I knew that by grinding Mr. Eliot into a fine dry powder and sprinkling that powder over Mr. Conrad's grave," Hemingway wrote in a letter, "Mr. Conrad would shortly appear, looking very annoyed at the forced return, and commence writing, I would leave for London tomorrow with a sausage grinder." Who else but someone with Hemingway's temperament would express the preference for one writer over another with such bluster and posturing? Most temperaments are not tolerant of other temperaments, and where differences are "sufficiently far-reaching," reason and logic are not going to wipe the sneer from the face or lower the temperature of the debate. In fact, heated argument is less about a point of order or scholarship than it is about the personalities and expectations of the combatants.

Take, for instance, the current debate regarding the place of art in society. Much has been said and written about the role of art, and much hoopla and attitudinizing have characterized the statements made by those who advocate art's autonomy and the so-called guardians of culture who hold art to a higher social and moral purpose. But what really is at stake here? Ultimately, argument involving questions of what is good or bad about art devolves into what is good or bad for society—in which case what we're really talking about is culture, or the aesthetic and moral standards that people identify with an *ideal* society. Thus, "culture" cannot be spoken *of* without its being spoken *for*. In a democratic, pluralistic society, culture is always "culture for whom?"—those who guard it? those who resent it? those who couldn't care less about it?

When Van Wyck Brooks, in 1915, wished to describe the reason that American culture had split into opposing factions of highbrowism and lowbrowism, he turned to the notion of personality. According to Brooks, the division began to occur in the eighteenth century with the appearance of Jonathan Edwards and Benjamin Franklin. Edwards displayed the "infinite inflexibility" of the upper levels of the American mind; Franklin, the "infinite flexibility" of its lower levels. The two states of mind were soon to be discerned in all areas of life: university ethics as opposed to business ethics, culture as opposed to humor, academic pedantry as opposed to pavement slang. America was being pulled toward "unmitigated theory" or "unmitigated practice," with neither position capable of appreciating the multiplicity found within a democratic society.

How does Brooks attempt to effect a reconciliation? "The only serious approach to society is the personal approach. . . . Personality will have to release itself on a middle plane between vaporous idealism and self-interested practicality." It is hard to know exactly what this means or how it can be enacted in the public realm. What is clear is that personality and politics are inextricably joined. Life itself is political, since politics exists as soon as the self recognizes the existence of another, independent self. In this overarching sense, politics underlies all human transactions and is, therefore, not a useful means to understand the sensibility and effort that go into making a poem, symphony, or painting. Although one can judge art by one's own political persuasions, one cannot, in this way, appreciate it for what it is, for surely if the work has aesthetic value, it possesses it *in addition* to whatever political creed it espouses or implicitly represents.

Yet those for whom politics and art cannot be divorced find

this point of view irrelevant, if not actually repugnant. To believe that man is in chains is to believe that some of the links are forged by culture—which explains why some professors claim that aesthetic terms such as "beauty," "order," "transcendence," and "quality" are, in reality, coercive strategies devised by a ruling class for the express purpose of maintaining distinctions between the privileged and the disenfranchised, in much the same way that certain "noble" emotions in classical tragedy were restricted to royalty.

There is nothing radical about this. The possession of culture, as Van Wyck Brooks observed, "has always been a jealous possession, it has the nature of a right which has been earned, an investment which might have been a yacht, a country-house, or a collection of Rembrandts instead." Indeed, there is nothing ambiguous about culture as regards the value it places on certain artifacts, but what degree of culpability attaches itself to this practice? Does it, in fact, consciously or unconsciously mean to keep down those who have not the means to participate in culture? Perhaps, but that is not the whole story. Aesthetic judgments—whatever their subliminal motives—also exist outside politics, just as the appreciation of skilled labor or trained musical voices exists apart from a political context.

Identifying art with the needs of the "people" in both totalitarian and free societies has the similarly unfortunate effect of reducing art to political agendas. In the middle of the nineteenth century, when certain critics condemned German lyric poetry for ignoring the starving masses, Heinrich Heine responded with a caustic verse: "Why sing of roses, you aristocrat? / Sing of the democratic potato, which keeps the people alive." One hopes that no one goes hungry, but when the democratic potato begins dictating to the rose, as now seems to be happening in American culture, it's going to be a poor garden in the spring.

Not all people feel strongly about art, and that is perfectly

reasonable. One might even say that people temperamentally disinclined to reflect seriously on their existence (though they may
expatiate at great length on how to conduct ourselves while in
existence) will probably not set great store by art. The temperament consumed by the injustices of the world will also show little
inclination to study the intelligence and craft that go into making a
work of art. For if what we mean by art connotes the awareness of
the limits that artists work with, limits imposed by their pre-
decessors and those innate to the medium itself, then art cannot be
understood without knowing how tradition both restricts and ex-
pands aesthetic possibilities.

True, no law of nature, or of human nature, dictates how each
of us must appreciate the fact of limits or what significance we
attach to them. For some people, death, gravity, and metaphysics
are beside the point except when they fall ill or board an airplane.
More crucial matters await their attention. No time to think about
the existential questions that paralyze romantic heroes. The truth
is, people busy apologizing for capitalism or Marxism, and people
deeply engaged in living as capitalists or Marxists, will probably
not have a metaphysical cast to their thinking. People who faith-
fully watch soap operas, who routinely call in to radio sports
shows, who eagerly await the newest Harlequin Romance, will
probably not be the best readers of Shakespeare. There is nothing terrible in that. In fact, not to acknowledge the importance
of philosophy and Shakespeare in one's life is also not to suffer
their absence.

No one is prevented from speaking about art, and no one, not
even an artist, has an absolute right to pronounce what is and isn't
art. It is only when art is held to standards unconcerned with
aesthetic matters that it becomes a focal point around which any
sort of ideological squabble may occur—a muddle that is no easier
for artists to avoid than for those temperamentally indifferent to
art. In fact, politics or the impulse to do "the right thing" may end

up influencing or interfering with artistic opinion. A case in point might be Leonard Bernstein, in 1968, opening his heart to the Beatles and his home to the Black Panthers. Both, one might argue, were in the nature of a political act. Bernstein probably did like the Beatles, but just as probably he liked them for more than their music. Still, this is better than disliking the Beatles merely because they represent in one's mind the liberal ethos of the Sixties. I won't argue the point, because one can no more argue a person into liking the Beatles than into liking a glass of beer, or into liking the Brandenburg Concertos if one doesn't happen to care for Bach. But, unlike Mr. Holmes, I do not think that a person's likes and dislikes, or two people's opinions, are equally sound.

The temptation to see this as nothing more than a *reductio ad absurdum* argument is to miss the point. If temperament explains why people argue, it does not assign a value to specific arguments. Indeed, an individual guided by temperament to the exclusion of all else—that is, someone devoid of an imaginative sympathy for other ways of seeing and describing—is not to be trusted. And anyone who writes about art must take care to be cognizant of temperament in order to keep his wits about him. "When I come across some profound piece of criticism into which the critic has, I feel, been led by surrendering to his own temperament," Desmond MacCarthy bravely wrote, "I wonder if my own method of criticizing is not mistaken. One cannot get away from one's temperament any more than one can jump away from one's shadow, but one can discount the emphasis which it produces. I snub my own temperament when I think it is not leading me straight to the spot where a general panorama of an author's work is visible."

Of course, it is a matter of temperament whether one can understand one's own temperament and make allowances for it. But whether one resists it or surrenders to it, temperament is a receiver, a way of absorbing information, a radar grid that picks up the darting, indistinct shapes of experience, which become

emotionally fused in the mind depending on the mind's predisposition. If this is true, as I believe it is, then why should not one
temperament be more suited than another to comprehending the
nature of art? And given art's strangely elusive nature, is not the
best temperament for the job the one that resonates to William
James's own final words: "What has concluded that we should
conclude in regard to it?"

[1988]

9

Art and Craft

istah Conrad—he dead. Well, yes. Conrad died in
1924, but he also died a second death during the
1970s when the author, or rather the idea of the Author, suffered an untimely demise. Although not the
first time that the work took precedence over the worker (at midcentury the New Criticism insisted on the separation of poem
and poet), this latest incarnation of the text's primacy was particularly despotic, in both a philosophical and political sense.
Literary movements, however, come and go, and the doctrines
that rudely deposited authors into their conceptual coffins—I
mean, the semiotic/deconstructionist writings of Barthes, Derrida,
Kristeva, et al.—are today deader than both Conrad and Kurtz.
Nonetheless, this attempt to limit the author's sovereignty was not
rejected without producing some lasting consequences.

As readers of literary criticism know, about thirty years ago
there occurred an inversion between the author and the work, and
between reader and writer that, in effect, amounted to a way of
discussing books based on the text's indefiniteness. A book could
propagate any number of serious discussions, but no discussion

could be serious without acknowledging the impossibility of *really* knowing what the writer intended. And, truth to tell, from a purely logical standpoint not all the academic arguments brought to bear on the text's self-referentiality were specious. And yet something did not sit right. Logic alone does not comprehend the making or the effect of art, and all that mummery about signifier and referent managed to overlook an inconvenient yet basic fact: someone put in the time and effort to create the artifact whose existence now served as a pretext to dismiss its maker.

Labor is finally responsible for works of art; if not for labor, every talented person would be an artist. What is required is work, and what is wanted is craft: the knowledge and the skill to make something. Indeed, in everything we do, whether it's planning dinner, building bridges, composing a villanelle, mixing a drink, or belting out a song or a triple, craft is necessary. Without it, the artistic temperament, to cite G. K. Chesterton, "is a disease which afflicts amateurs." For the literary artist, making something is a way of arriving at a thought or emotion that might otherwise never be spoken. Artists "speak" in music, paint, stone, or dance because their sense of life finds expression in a particular medium, and they continue to speak because this sense of life is always changing. If the world, as Keats thought, is "The vale of Soul-making," then the craft of poetry is both the process and the record of that making. As it is with all art forms.

But how does one assess the craft that informs literary labor? By sweat? By tears? By the hours one spends composing and refining the work? None of these seems an appropriate measure. After all, one poet's glorious work of two years may be achieved by a more gifted poet in two months. Craft, then, is not so much a unit of energy as the product of expectations formed by the artist's own experience, a deliberate wish to make something in one way and not another. Craft is—it cannot be otherwise—an extension of personality, residing in the tension between temperament and the manner in which temperament expresses itself. In some cases, the exposition tilts toward the formal; in others, toward the confessional, depending on how the writer chooses to balance personal revelation with the sometimes oppositional urge to challenge tradition.

"The more perfect the artist," wrote an exemplary craftsman, "the more completely separate in him will be the man who suffers and the mind which creates." But this—Eliot's resurrection of Nietzsche's self-conscious artist—is really nothing more than the attitude of a young man who has not lived enough and who still believes that art should aspire to "a continual extinction of personality." In time, Eliot would reverse direction, conceding that his suffering and his art could not be separated.

In short, no art without craft; no craft without individual sensibility; and no art-object without the artist's negotiation between tradition and innovation. To rephrase Eliot's dictum: the more consummate the artist, the greater the burden in weighing the demands of form and content. Since no artist wishes to travel down roads already taken, the deliberations regarding how to proceed in light of what has come before can have the effect of making the work seem difficult or obscure.

The three novels of James Joyce come to mind. Clearly, Joyce was not a man who put craft at the service of clarity. When Max Eastman observed that he made too many demands on his readers, the author retorted: "The demand that I make of my reader is that he should devote his whole life to reading my works." One might be willing to oblige the old artificer up to a point, a point that for many readers comes at *Finnegans Wake,* a novel that wants decipherers rather than mere readers. Surely no other work of fiction or poetry (and *Finnegans* has been described as both) places the responsibility of reading so squarely on the head of the reader. No matter how much we may enjoy browsing in it, clearing aside the brush of words to get at the puns, references, and jokes, the whole thing shimmers with what can only be characterized as willful perversity.

The book is difficult, and yet its difficulty, if chastening, is also curiously heartening in these multicultural/gender-ridden days, when sentences possess neither beauty nor wisdom but only linguistic codes. For Joyce's much-vaunted and resented obscurity does not actually seem inherent in language or in the infinite subjectivities that may interpret it. Instead it derives from the determined mind of an Irishman named Joyce, a person we happen to know something about.

In terms of reputation, as a writer who must be dealt with before one can come to grips with modern literature, Joyce is the twentieth-century equivalent of Shakespeare—with one important difference. For centuries, Shakespeare has been a talismanic name, more creator than human creation. Knowing so little about him, we tend to regard the plays and sonnets as *sui generis,* almost as if there had never been an umbilical cord for the New Critics to snip off. Because there is no one there—no familiar individual with his peeves, obsessions, and recorded impressions—critics, over the years, have felt free to reinvent the oeuvre.

They will not be so lucky with Joyce. Joyce bends over his writings, the words glinting off his spectacles and dropping from his nicotine-stained fingers. No chance of removing him from the work; indeed, he makes his life a precondition of understanding the work, and this is being confirmed all the time by the biographies, journals, letters, and the memoirs of people who knew him. The reputation may fade, but the writer will not, and any attempt to interpret the work without tackling the writer will be an act so irresponsible as to border on the foolish. The temperament, the personality, the tastes of James Joyce have been, as much as such things can be, documented. And simply because such documentation is not available in the case of Shakespeare does not make it any less relevant. *Someone* wrote the plays and poems, and he is

entitled to the same consideration given to writers whose lives we
know something about. This may seem absurd in light of the
missing biographical material, but what is really at issue here?
How we might imagine the plays or what the author meant for us
to understand by them? Shakespeare's motives and meanings may
not always be clear, but those that can be gleaned from the works
are enough to demonstrate that we cannot simply tack on significance where none was intended.

The cautionary note that pertains to Joyce applies equally to
Shakespeare: There is an intelligence at work. Given this
fact, is it really a daring act of theory to place a wreath on the idea
of the Author? Isn't the presumption, in fact, a less interesting and
less subtle reality than the author's continued existence? The Author's demise does not, as Barthes thinks, achieve the birth of the
reader, but only the birth of the metacritic, and surely there have
been happier begettings. Nor is it particularly enlightening to regard the Author as a logocentric construct (what word isn't?); as
for the term being a code word for ideological tyrant, as some
critics would have it, one can only suggest that the political content
of literature, while greater than that in rum cake, is still a matter of
degree. Politics is simply a part of everything we do and think.

When we put our faith in a writer's conscious or unconscious
intentions, we do not automatically create a false God who must be
disavowed. The creator of novels or poems was never in the minds
of most readers the absolute authority that the metacritics now
claim, not even an absolute that somehow managed to go un-
noticed. The flesh-and-blood writer was, in fact, known to be
more complicated than Barthes's "Author," and the work more
complicated than the signs and systems now equated with the text.
Literature is complicated because, as Lionel Trilling wrote, "literature is not an exception to the conditioned nature of things: it is

what it is by reason of the circumstances of its genesis, which are the circumstances, both external and internal, of the man who made it; and he, in turn, no less than the things he creates, is a conditioned being susceptible to explanation in terms of the circumstances that determined his nature."

The cultural complicity of literature about which ideologues make such a fuss is taken for granted by Trilling. But because literature is not primarily a political act, though it implicitly reflects political bias, and writers like George Orwell may openly treat political matters and movements, literature's accomplishment cannot be viewed solely against a political backdrop. Like any art, literature is both the cause and result of an evolving sensibility, whose practitioners depend on their knowledge of art in order to create new art, and what they know depends on the circumstances, both external and internal, that define them.

There is a reason that certain works, even if they fall in and out of critical favor over the years, last—and it is not merely that an educated elite insists on setting the standards. But to appreciate the reason, we must allow that artists have a definite aesthetic purpose in mind, that this purpose characterized their labor long before "aesthetic" became a term associated with the arts, and that since the dawn of civilization artists have shared a temperamental disposition to represent reality in concrete form. It is not enough for such a temperament merely to think, imagine, or feel; it must transform itself in work. So before it is anything else, art is an artifact, a product of labor; and as in all kinds of labor there are individuals who work harder and better than others—which is why no artist, at any rate, condones the notion that the things he or she makes, or comparable things made by others, are all equally well made.

Because no artist wishes merely to reproduce what has already been done, he must first acquaint himself with the tradition he works in. Because the serious artist wishes to be neither the same as, nor less than, other artists, the work always looks backward by virtue of its refusal to be merely imitative. That is, it necessarily occupies a designated slot in the temporal scheme of things. On this score, the New Historicists are certainly correct. Nonetheless, this temporality (whether we refer to it as tradition or progress) helps define art as the product of other art, and helps enrich our appreciation of the standards the artist encountered and those he created in grappling with preexisting standards.

This intent, in a word, identifies the difference between high and low art. The former pays homage to tradition while also rebelling against it. Popular art has a more simplistic relation to what preceded it: it capitalizes on past success, content to repeat it, doing little to alter or improve it. So when an academic press in 1991, touting still another book blurring the distinction between high and low, asks the question, "From *King Lear* to *King Kong*, from *Daniel Deronda* to *Gone with the Wind*—are the differences really so great?" one may answer "yes," even if one has a soft spot for Margaret Mitchell. For when it comes to popular culture, there is (never mind what the audience wants) less knowledge on the part of the creator, less work, lower expectations, and inevitably a feebler result.

T he idea of standards may be inherent in the human condition. A "standard" is something, as my *American Heritage Dictionary* notes, "that under specified conditions defines, represents, or records the magnitude of a unit." Broadly speaking, we are all units, and the specified condition unique to us, and unconditionally shared by all of us, which "defines, represents, or records" us, is time. Mortality is a standard: it measures us, it takes our measure, and it puts limits on either side of existence. What is a person if not a limited affair with existence? Limits define us, they are the standards that represent and record us, and naturally they disturb us. Who wants to be limited?

In the case of artists, the limits they seek to transcend are twofold: the limits set by precursors who have managed to paint, write, or compose in a style that makes further efforts seem superfluous, and the limits of the human condition itself, which restrict the artist's time on earth as well as his consciousness of time. The artistic temperament is one that is acutely aware of both standards: those created by precursors and those inherent in life itself. In both instances, the recognition of temporality summons forth the efforts that mean to understand and transcend these limits. There is nothing remotely mystical or vatic in this definition of artistic labor; it suggests only a clear-eyed view of the struggle that all conscious beings who wish to make their intelligence concrete in artistic form are engaged in.

The problem today is that too many people fancy themselves, or are identified as, "artists." Because art does volume business these days—it's everywhere and just about everything made in its name is deemed worthy—the idea of art has become unmoored. Where once art was more or less recognized by those who could appreciate the craft that went into it, today the mere willingness to make art seems sufficient to justify the effort. Thus painters without a gift for drawing, artists who conceptualize rather than paint or sculpt, and poets who seem unaware of prosody all have license to create. But create what? Igor Stravinsky referred to such people as engaging in "the common heresy," and it was not one that he was prepared to condone. "In art as in everything else," he wrote, "you can build only upon a firm resisting foundation, and everything that resists you must likewise restrict your freedom of motion. So my liberty consists in moving inside the narrow bounds within which I set myself for each thing I undertake."

One does not, therefore, have to approve of every word that

Homer sang or Shakespeare wrote to know that they practiced their crafts better than did their contemporaries. Like the cushion that Gibbon rested his gouty leg on, Shakespeare too provides a support; he is what we depend on to know how well or ill other writers have performed; he is what we depend on when we forget and want reminding of who we are.

But the conditioned nature of things, to borrow Trilling's phrase, conspires against a definition of art that is fixed and inviolable. A human being is not an unchanging sum; and the writer, that epitome of self-consciousness, ever alert to a change in the tally, is the first to acknowledge such impermanence. It is one reason he writes, in the hope that writing will make him complete. A vain hope perhaps, but if the resulting work is genuine—original in form and arresting in content—then he or she at least has the satisfaction of knowing that the work is a measure of other works within the genre.

The metacritics argue, however, that mind has not the capacity, nor language the skeleton, for absolute knowledge. Consequently, we have no business creating standards and rewarding or punishing artists insofar as they meet or fail to meet these standards. By putting the emphasis on the fallibility of aesthetic criteria, because of either cognitive or political tendencies, such critics believe they have made the case against the canon of Great Books. But how is it possible *not* to judge works of art? If one accepts that art is a product of mind and execution, it is immediately apparent that not all artists perform equally well.

Instead of uncertainty and indeterminacy presenting readers with *carte blanche* when judging art, they suggest just the opposite: the need for discrimination. Judgment—judgment about books, judgment about everything—is necessary precisely where knowledge is uncertain. Only in a world where mind and matter are evidentially in accord, where existence is synonymous with meaning, where one word comprises both theology and teleology, does the need for judgment disappear. Such a world, as most people will concede, is not quite the one we find ourselves in.

So we muddle on, discovering if not actively seeking our limitations. We look, listen, and ponder, reflecting why this novel and that painting move us, why they give pleasure, why they seem worthy of being remembered and returned to. The answers we proffer need not satisfy everyone; the point is that we need to ask the questions—questions demanded by the artists whose works insist on being judged. That, after all, is what the artist truly represents: someone who wishes to make him or herself known to us, a consciousness that intuits from experience what might reasonably be expressed in form, a form that will engage another consciousness. We owe it to the intelligence that creates art to judge the work; to do less is to dismiss the intelligence that made it.

[1988]

10

Certitudes

———

Certainty can be exhilarating; uncertainty, never. There is something fundamentally disquieting about not knowing the truth of things, the real as opposed to the unreal, the facts as opposed to the theories. Admittedly, artists and intellectuals occasionally celebrate uncertainty as if it were a liberating cause, but in the end uncertainty holds no thrill for me. Pliny's maxim that "There is nothing certain but uncertainty, and nothing more miserable and arrogant than man" possesses the very quality the statement means to disparage. I reserve judgment about uncertainty, just as I would about anything that cannot be demonstrated without fear of contradiction. Instead, I make a melancholy adjustment. Although every question is, at bottom, a sigh, some seem worth asking more than others: "What is certain?"

In a post-Humean, post-Wittgensteinian world, the question invites a knowing shrug. What is certain? Phenomenologically speaking, very little. We exist, but the precise forms that existence takes are not beyond logical doubt: not only do perceptions differ, but the brain itself refuses to process the same sensations in consistent fashion. Nor can we somehow fix on universal truths concerning ethics or human behavior. The Declaration of Independence notwithstanding, there are no self-evident truths that we are created equal and equally entitled to life, liberty, and the pursuit of happiness. It is pleasant to think so, and almost certainly better to live in a country that holds to these beliefs, but such sentiments are not absolute truths that have somehow managed to escape the attention of previous ages or other cultures. Whatever the physical world is *really* like is a formulation that can never be demonstrated without some element of doubt creeping in. But if uncertainty characterizes the relation between matter and how we view matter, it is in the end more of a conceit about our own limitations than a guiding principle of behavior. Basically we get along quite well under its sovereign stare. Like Dr. Johnson, we habitually refute the uncertainty of inductive reasoning by kicking aside whatever logical stones cross our path.

Nevertheless, the idea of uncertainty has its appeal, and its consequences—most notably when we transform it into a fashionable nihilism. Currently, such fashion decrees that traditional western values regarding art, morality, and society, being political rather than intrinsic to human nature, exist under a cognitive cloud that we have only recently spotted. One may think of this cloud as having been formed during the Enlightenment, when philosophy, broadly speaking, still held to the belief that knowledge validly derived by one person is valid for all people. Even while acknowledging the gulf between what *is* and what is *perceived*, Enlightenment philosophers thought that mind (via language) could bridge this gulf—that, in fact, universal principles of art and life existed in the very commutation between thought and expression, principles that could be applied productively to human affairs.

Needless to say, such assurances did not survive the first quarter of the twentieth century, when language philosophers made short work of the empirical link between words and the phe-

nomena they signified; reality, whatever it was, was unknowable
and certainly incapable of being represented in any absolute sense.
This being so, artists and writers were absolved from seeking a
deeper meaning in phenomena. Instead, they were free to look
within themselves or else to rearrange things in any way they saw
fit, since reality literally had no truth to speak of.

Still, the ideal of art, of a progressive development in form,
style, and perspective, was not devalued. However much the modernist movement, in its initial phase, deviated from traditional ways
of doing art, it did not renounce the idea of art's collective history.
Writers and artists continued to see themselves as part of a tradition, accepting the duty of climbing aesthetic ladders before kicking them aside. In fact, a defining element of modernism was its
self-conscious attitude toward the past, an awareness of its historical situation, which was a natural extension of nineteenth-century
preoccupations with the study of history. In this self-conscious
regard, the modernism of Eliot, Pound, Joyce, Picasso, Gropius,
Brancusi, and Stravinsky knew itself to be the last, *though not final,*
stage of an aesthetic tradition that began with the Enlightenment's
conception of art as something made especially for intellectual
contemplation.

In retrospect, the next stage appears inevitable. To establish
their own identities, succeeding generations of artists borrowed
the concept of philosophical and scientific uncertainty that was
already part of the modernist charter (though not the most important part) and exploited it in order to invalidate modernism itself.
Obviously, the wholesale rejection of aesthetic tradition is nascent
in a cognitive system that holds out no hope for absolute truth or
universally valid principles of judgment. So brandishing (and often
misunderstanding) the writings of Wittgenstein, Freud, Einstein,
and Heisenberg, artists in the second half of the twentieth century
saw themselves as purveyors of the murky unconscious as well as
seers of the familiar and superficial—concerns evident in abstract

expressionism, atonal music, unstructured confessional poetry, present-tense fiction, indeed in all work that willfully deviates from traditional perspectives.

As established philosophical models fell by the academic way-side, and the old debates about God, man and reality came to an end, the arts—peremptorily sensing the intellect's tenuous con-nection with truth—put aside realism and representation in order to express the new, fragmented, uncertain, unsignifiable universe. Briefly, during the modernist period, artists thought to replace the lost certainties of the nineteenth century with the ideal of art itself—a more social-minded incarnation of the art-for-art's-sake movement of the *belle époque*—hoping to fashion autonomous works not beholden to a generally accepted view of external reality. But modernism's center could not hold. Art fell prey to the skepti-cism that now attached itself to all ideals: art was not one true thing; it could be anything, and anything could be art.

Without that confidence in a truer and deeper reality residing behind appearances, artists naturally shifted their attention to the appearances themselves. Surfaces were now reexamined as "sur-faces" whose meaning had been misplaced or ignored; the obvious was more than obvious, and everything ordinary became worthy of serious study. Profundity did not disappear from the earth, it was merely transposed onto its face; and, as if to compensate for the loss of truly meaningful issues, the criticism that accompanied this shift aspired to an intellectual height that towered over its mun-dane subject matter. Witness this 1980s catalogue description of a well-received exhibition at a SoHo art gallery: "In this recent series . . . the sign is curved, a dialectical 3, eluding the necessity of either blandness or insight. It tries to slip through the cracks which separate the modernist authenticity of authorial production and the postmodern collapse of the project of meaning. . . . [The artist] transforms a category, which first appears in Lévi-Strauss's analysis of the myth-maker *bricoleur,* into a reversal of a determinate set in the production of meaning."

What is the critic heatedly trying to convince us of here? Essentially that a series of rather insipid paintings featuring the numeral 3 now fills the intellectual space vacated by traditional philosophy. Put another way: the secret of everyday objects and symbols—of what is constantly before us and taken for granted—is that such things are charged with powerful significance. Some years ago, a photograph of a famous photograph evoked considerable discussion as to which was the real art-object. If postmodern art is the perfect expression of an antimetaphysical bias, one might also suggest that where philosophy is absent, art speaks not of, but within, the void. Instead of having intrinsic meaning, such art possesses only the theoretical significance accorded it by academicians.

Bad art, of course, has always outnumbered the good, but now something new has been added to the mix. Bad art is no longer considered "bad" in the sense that it falls short of established criteria. Indeed, the very idea of quality has come under fire. On July 22, 1990, readers of the *New York Times* were treated to an article titled: "Is 'Quality' an Idea Whose Time Has Gone?" which suggested that quality is part of that white, male, Eurocentric conspiracy that has historically neglected the situation of women, minorities, and the disenfranchised. While the *New York Times* critic sidestepped the issue of judging the argument's merits, it is obvious that many writers, critics, and artists have decided that quality is an elitist lens ground by those with a vested interest in the sale and promotion of art. Apparently, in a better world, where one's vision had been corrected, the idea of quality would be consigned to the refuse heap of such inherently prejudicial notions as the divine right of kings and racial superiority.

It is, of course, neither illegal nor immoral to disparage art, but it does seem illogical to look at a stack of white paper with the same bland aphorism on every sheet and call it "art." Either one retains the idea of art as something that transcends the familiar, or one changes the meaning of the word, in which case it is possible to place an exhibition of paint-splattered plastic chairs in the same category as Michelangelo's *Pietà*. Endorsing bad art, after all, is but a short step from saying that no art is also art, which is as old as Dada; and given what Duchamp and Company intended with their urinals and bicycles, surely we must recognize that after the first Dada there can be no other.

Superficially, there may be nothing wrong with allowing that all artistic creations are worthy of respect. Such a position has a nice democratic ring to it. But even where the enforced absence of standards has precedence, critics undermine their own egalitarian pose by attributing to contemporary works a significance that seems strangely at odds with the works themselves. Only someone who has been utterly bamboozled by academic gibberish could not know that the popular novels, movies, and art-objects heralded by the critics are really fatuous, shallow, and dull works into which precious little work has gone. Sadly, neither learning nor skill nor toil—never mind genius—is now required to produce art; and the significant art of our day is art that comments on its own antitraditional virtues, that finds "the aesthetic" both philosophically and politically suspect. To the degree that this perspective defines artistic and critical approaches, contemporary art is at bottom antimodernist, which is to say that it is anti-art, which is really what postmodernism is all about.

One may, of course, without casuistry, make the case that art, being the reflection of its age, is only as authentic as the age requires it to be. If the age demands antinomian works which reflect dissatisfaction with what God and man have so far intended for humanity and wrought on its behalf, including the idea of ultimate ethical and metaphysical meaning, then we do, indeed, have the culture we deserve. On the other hand, one may regard the art of today as simply inadequate to the task of revealing the deeper levels, the bedrock truths that are no less true today than in the past. If, as I've suggested, there are no certainties in this life, since a certainty, strictly speaking, admits no possibility of evidence contrary to it, there still may be truths that we can acknowledge without insisting on their absolute certainty, facts that all individuals, whatever their religious orientation and temperament, must agree on—namely, the physical dimension of our bodies, the physical forces acting on them, and the end of the physical.

Truth, in short, consists of the body, gravity (or some force that binds us to the earth), and death. And it is the truth of these three things that art, philosophy, and religion mean to circumvent by positioning other truths alongside them. What else are all our ideas and revelations but schemes to outwit these unflinching truths? Such additional hopeful certainties are invented precisely because the triumvirate fact of body/gravity/death is patently not enough. Inadequacy, reluctant though we may be to admit it, is a fair description of the human condition. We are inadequate because we do not live forever; life itself is inadequate because it cannot demonstrate that there should be something rather than nothing. And however one is disposed to regard death's "finality," at the very least it means the end of that physical existence we know to be uniquely our own.

So even if there are no moral or revealed truths that all people can agree on, the truth of a shared mortality connects them. For Socrates, philosophy was "the practice of dying," by which he meant that death is what makes philosophy possible. We brood on existence, and yet there is no guarantee that pondering the great themes of life and death will make them any clearer. A great one for brooding, Heidegger eventually concluded that the "finite and limited character of human existence is more primordial than man himself." Man is not the mystery: the mystery is that any being should exist at all, that existence itself should exist. For Heidegger, this intimation is at the heart of all thought. Like Socrates, he felt that mortality ultimately determines how we think, and that coming to grips with our accidental and physical selves is what induces us to philosophize about what is good, beautiful, true, and what is not.

To philosophize about such matters assumes a belief in language's ability not only to define ideas but to signify in a meaningful way the existence of physical objects, even if only as viable referents within language. Such faith, we have been told, is misguided. Because the relation between the sign and its referent is arbitrary, a convenient myth, philosophy must distrust the only means at its disposal (symbolic logic excepted) with which to talk about the world. And consequently those ageless questions about fate, free will, purpose, and man's lot in a protean cosmos have been shelved along with other "antiquarian" notions and theories.

With the collapse of determinate meaning in art came the end of aesthetic validation. Artworks came to be seen primarily as cultural artifacts, mirroring the political and psychological beliefs and values of the day. And the art that now began to flourish (and which still flourishes) took its justification from openly embracing political and social agendas. Such is the current climate: shallow art and academic criticism play off one another, and neither seems willing to acknowledge the troublesome fact that the human condition is remarkably resistant to all attempts to ignore it. The mystery of existence, after all, does not grow appreciably clearer because theorists decide to emphasize one aspect of it over another. The human condition, for good or ill, remains one of unalterable limitation.

We are limited, finite beings, whose intellectual aspirations have always taken the form of self-justifying and self-consoling patterns of thought that mean to transcend the very limitations that motivate these thoughts. Who can doubt it? We are at the mercy of time and gravity; and the possibility of thought itself seems impossible without a body to sustain it. Both our mental and physical universes extend from the stationary object that is the body and, as the Ancients knew, one cannot speak of human nature without speaking of the body. And the body is temporary. So for all that daily life occupies us, for all that our parents, spouses, lovers, and children distract us, for all that the world's problems disturb us, we are still beings who walk upright on a mass of rock that spins around a burning core of gaseous matter, in a solar system that is but a speck in a galaxy that is itself rushing along with a billion others into black, limitless space. The only knowledge more astonishing than this is the knowledge that one day such knowledge will end.

Death limits us; it limits us to a definite, if unknown, amount of time on earth; and time itself defines the periods of our growth from infancy to maturity to old age. Meanwhile, gravity coupled with our spatial dimensions puts limits on the body's physical powers. And if our bodies have anything to teach us, surely the fact of limits—of beginnings, middles, and ends—is part of the lesson.

We live with and within limits. How we isolate objects in the mind, how we see, hear, speak, and write are all contingent on the fact that we perceive in four dimensions, not five or eight or twenty. The very idea of civilization is one of limits; it limits anarchy and aggression. Every word we invent limits the meaning of every other word. Art, too, has its limits, and those who demand an art without standards (standards being, in fact, limits) might as well be advocating the climbing of sheer rock without rope and pitons. Without standards, art becomes unhinged, just as spontaneous, unruled expression necessarily devolves into confusion. A hundred people "creating," or "acting out," as the psychiatrists might say, in any manner they choose, soon enough manifest gibberish. All their gestures, words, paintings, all the expressions of their unique personalities will become in short order indistinguishable from one another. Instead of expressing individuality, such license succeeds only in blurring individuality, without which art is meaningless.

True, no law of nature, or law of human nature, dictates how each of us must appreciate the limitations that mortality imposes, but this much at least is true: we die, and such truth—indeed, any truth—in a manner of speaking, limits. If one thing is *absolutely* the case, other things are not the case. The most basic human truth is that human beings are locked into and limited by their physical bodies, which sooner or later are emptied of consciousness. And a corollary of this truth is that art, being a product of defined spatial and temporal beings, is limited as well. Artists, therefore, have a duty to perform, part of which is to recognize the limits that confront them. "There is no freedom in art," declared T. S. Eliot— a statement not meant to circumscribe the possibilities in art, for who can list all the possible correspondences that exist between thought and expression? What Eliot knew about poetry is what all thoughtful people know about living in the world: "freedom is only truly freedom when it appears against the background of an artificial limitation."

[1988]

11

What Happened?
The Rise and Fall of Theory

———

Not so long ago, though it may seem that way, literary criticism was practiced by people for whom literature was essential to thinking about life. Such people wrote about books in order to write about art, politics, religion, and the interaction of society and culture—in short, what men and women of letters have always brought to the table. Although the same can be said of current literary practitioners, something else can be said as well: Unlike those who interpret books today, earlier critics possessed an implicit belief in literature's significance, not simply because literature espoused a point of view, but because the language it used was a language that existed for writers before it could exist for readers—in much the same way that melodies exist for us only after composers hear them and transcribe them as musical notes. Literary critics of forty years ago, even if their own articulate musings were less memorably phrased than the poems and novels they wrote about, paid homage to such works by mining the same rich vein of language.

One sometimes forgets just how interesting and well-written literary criticism used to be. To read Leavis, Blackmur, Eliot,

Trilling, Tate, Winters, and Jarrell; to read Desmond MacCarthy, V. S. Pritchett, Irving Howe, Philip Rahv, F. W. Dupee, and Alfred Kazin (William Empson and Kenneth Burke are special cases)— whether or not one agrees with them—is to read critics for whom literature necessarily preceded criticism and who felt no misgivings about professing their veneration for the literary endeavor. Part of the job description for the intellectuals of another day was a familiarity with contemporary poems and novels. The appearance of a new work by Faulkner, Hemingway, Nabokov, or the young Saul Bellow was certain to engage the likes of Edmund Wilson, Jacques Barzun, and W. H. Auden. No one confused the creative work with that of the critical, but at least the two were thought to play on the same field. And though many of these critics eventually ended up as academics themselves, and perhaps inadvertently helped to bring about the shift in American letters from literary journalism to academic criticism, none, I think, truly imagined the chasm that would one day open up between the literary and the intellectual life in America.

Today, the title of intellectual is not synonymous with that of writer or man of letters. Today, the intellectual is an academic or a professor, and professors of literature, as they will be the first to acknowledge, are quite superior to the text in hand. They have to be, given that novels and poems are semiotic tracts that reflect all sorts of nasty, royalist, elitist, patriarchal, sexist, and imperialist sympathies. In most cases, the "greatness" of a work is sufficient cause for its diminution, since its very reputation as a classic makes it suspect. Hence, the classic novels, poems, and plays must be brought down to size, scaled down to the biases and ignorance of the artist and the age that produced them. This makes for happy academics, but a rather bewildered audience. When reading contemporary criticism, it is difficult to find anywhere in it a true feeling for literature, the sense that some poems and some novels have deeply affected the critic in a passionate or spiritual sense.

The mangled prose in academic journals, whether its subject is Melville's *Billy Budd* or Shelley's *Ozymandias,* cannot be said to reflect a love for the language that produced such works. And when critics begin to regard literature as a spool around which to wrap the more precious thread of explication, readers hoping to understand their own response to novels and poems are going to come away empty.

Language and thought are inseparable: how we speak about things is a sign of how we think, and when critics speak like sociologists or political philosophers, they are speaking a language unequipped to appreciate the act or fact of literature. Reading such criticism one may recall Shaw's devastating one-sentence indictment of Christianity's evolution: "There has really never been a more monstrous imposition perpetrated than the imposition of the limitation of Paul's soul upon the soul of Jesus." What happened to bring about such a change in the way we talk about literature?

What happened was this: With the gravitation of writers to the university, starting in the Fifties, a change in the respective status of creative writing and criticism began to occur. Officially encouraged to create literature, writers sputtered. Officially encouraged to develop theory, critics flourished. While writers and poets found a sinecure in the halls of academe, which enabled them to write increasingly clever and self-referential works not intended for popular consumption, the professors began to rethink critical assumptions and the social context in which literary criticism had taken root. Regarding literature primarily as just one more form of written discourse, these professors, variously known as deconstructionists, poststructuralists, or metacritics, went on to discover the text's imprisonment in language. Their conclusion? No legitimate correlation could be made between the truth outside books and the complicated sign-systems within them.

With the collapse of determinate meaning in art came the end of aesthetic validation. Art works were now seen primarily as cultural artifacts, inevitably reflecting—and limited by—the political temper, moral values, and linguistic/psychological systems of the day, which, by definition, could not hope to transcend the society that formed them. Accordingly, the base of literary criticism not only broadened but sprouted a philosophical umbrella that gave shade to the various interest groups for whom the idea of Western culture is a conceit devised by the few to subjugate the many. In effect, the postmodern ethos disclaims the aesthetic history that led up to it, or shifts the emphasis from the art-object to the ways we talk about it. Literature itself had become the center that is somehow beside the point.

To those toiling in the academy, the infusion of theory was like a shot of vitamin B; not only did it invigorate them, it made them see better. Those hallowed works, the Great Books, with their Old Testament-like authority, were evidentiary sign-systems waiting to be deconstructed. But disillusionment counts for little if not accompanied by revelation. So not only were formerly accepted models of objectivity put aside, but a new and more "sophisticated" paradigm took their place, which basically stated that sentient beings are condemned by their neurological make-up and by the self-referential limits of language to read and write in a manner not verifiable by a reality external to the act of thinking. In short, our mental operations are precisely what make certainty impossible.

Not that this was exactly news in philosophical circles. Inductive reasoning without benefit of divine guidance to back up perception was always considered to be an inconclusive—i.e., nonabsolute—way of knowing the world, at least until Kant's introduction of synthetic a priori judgments. Still, what the poststructuralists succeeded in doing was to apply this epistemological tease to literature. By insisting that books could be interpreted only by theorists acutely aware, as Paul de Man would have it, of the "hidden

articulations and fragmentations within assumedly monadic total-
ities," academic critics began to reverse previously accepted relations between literature and criticism and between reader and
writer; in short time criticism became immaculately conceived; no
actual works of literature were necessary to engender it.

   This is heady stuff, and I don't mind admitting that it put some
life into a tired literature curriculum from which philosophical ideas
were mostly absent. Theory was tough, turgid, troublesome, but
also interesting. Intimidating to many, it was also fair intellectual
game, especially for critics with a background in philosophy. In any
case, it was new and had to be dealt with. Semiotic-, hermeneutic-,
deconstructionist-, anxiety-influence-, reader-response-, feminist-,
ethnicist-, and psychoanalytic-based approaches, as well as the
writings of the Prague School, the Frankfurt School, and the Russian Formalists, were grist for the mill, ink for the pen.

   And what happened was this: the people whose job it was to
evaluate literary works could no longer be bothered to read contemporary novels and poems or, for that matter, many of the Great
Books of the past. Stendhal and Sainte-Beuve became relics, purveyors of language innocent of its own implications. To decon-
struct this "innocence," professors of literature (many of whom
had no real grounding in philosophy) were suddenly poring over
the works of Heidegger, Benjamin, Adorno, Derrida, de Man,
Foucault, Lacan, Bakhtin, and half a dozen other thinkers. And if
the price of losing one's own innocence was submitting to the
technical, jargon-ridden, and clumsy ("valorizing," "foreground-
ing," "commodifying") language of academic discourse—well,
that was the price one had to pay. To be taken seriously, critics had
to acknowledge, by difficult example, that the problematic nature
of mind and language required a correspondingly involuted and
complicated discourse. And so what the party line basically came
down to was this: "There are texts of theory that resist meaning so
powerfully—say those by Lacan or Kristeva—that the very process

of failing to comprehend the text is part of what it has to offer" (Frank Lentricchia and Thomas McLaughlin, eds., *Critical Terms for Literary Study*, 1990). Does this mean that the more one doesn't understand, the more the text has to offer?

With the prevailing intellectual temper opposed to the idea of standards, and with academic presses midwifing one book after another upholding the primacy of popular culture over high culture, is it any wonder that no one expects very much in the way of literary excellence? And when I contemplate this, I begin to miss the deconstructionists. They, at least, were formidable intellectual opponents, whose arguments were, in point of fact, as irrefutable as Berkeley's refutation of matter, or Hume's of causation. However one felt about it, deconstruction presented a rallying point for readers who saw in it an intellectual dragon that breathed real fire, whose very existence made the interpretation and, hence, the appreciation of literature a stimulating if open-ended polemic. You could argue with a deconstructionist about whether poetry is "the foreknowledge of criticism," but what could you say to someone who maintained that Yeats was not worth reading because of his attitude toward women?

Anyway, such arguments by the end of the 1980s were futile. Theory had won. By whittling away at concepts of objectivity and value for twenty years, the professors had undermined the belief in aesthetic validity, thus enabling criticism of a frankly political cast to enter the curriculum. Aesthetics had become one more manifestation of ideology, which, by insisting on making discriminations, is seen to be roughly parallel to a capitalist system that differentiates among social classes. Having discovered that Western civilization is a conspiracy of the few to subjugate the many, academic critics quickly hit on the remedy: flatten out the intellectual terrain until all people can travel easily across it. As a result, works of art are interpreted semiotically, politically, culturally, and sexually—every which way but aesthetically. And if quality falls by the wayside, all to the good, since the idea of "quality" itself is politically suspect.

If anything good can be said to have come from theorists bent on pulling the aesthetic rug out from under our feet, it is that such critics have prompted others to reassert the historical particularity of reading. Art does recapitulate ideology—something that the self-professed aesthete forgets at his or her peril. "There is no escape from contingency," pronounced Stephen Greenblatt; no "formal textual autonomy, no numinous literary authority, only the product of collective negotiation and exchange." Quite so, and who ever said otherwise? Although the New Critics chose to focus on content rather than context, who among them actually believed that art arises in some sort of formal vacuum? For similar reasons, even an inveterate opponent of theory must acknowledge that art is the product of place, time, and culture. To press home the point, Terry Eagleton tells us that "literature," as we know it, shines through the prism of romanticism and modernism and is resolutely, if not always recognizably, ideological.

Yet when has it been otherwise? Did not such critics as Lionel Trilling, M. H. Abrams, Georg Lukács, and George Steiner, each in his own way, connect the rise of the aesthetic movement, romanticism, and the novel with the consolidation of a bourgeois culture, with its emphasis on beauty, privacy, and collecting? If Eagleton insists on seeing in these very accoutrements the lesson that literature is never more than the great white middle-class hope, that alone does not restrict art to a proscribed set of beliefs or demonstrate that everything produced by a particular culture carries the same aesthetic or intellectual weight. The fact that bourgeois culture invested art with a strong hierarchical intent does not mean that art is without such intent. Anyway, the attempt to imprison art within an ideological framework is also ideological, and if theory strips art of the transcendent qualities that other ages saw in it, that is simply another form of ideology at work: the ascendance of a materialist/determinist bias over a more idealistic/aesthetic one.

What is most infuriating about all these antinomian theorists is their presumption that the rest of us hold to a permanent and implacable set of values, as if we're incapable of realizing that values must be reevaluated in light of changing historical conditions. Cannot intelligent and even leftist-leaning readers respect tradition while rejecting authority? The truth is, neither Eagleton's nor Greenblatt's admonitions present an obstacle to the reader intent on discovering which part of the literary universe beckons. And perhaps the saddest aspect of all this palaver about the arts is that it is being perpetrated by academics rather than by what used to be called public intellectuals. The recognizable writer-critic who lived for and, in part, by reading has all but disappeared. Aside from John Updike, whose graciousness to writers continues unabated, whom can we regularly turn to for news of the literary scene? Evidently, that task has fallen to those who read in order to identify the hidden fallacies and biases that words contain, and for whom the book is a psychological hieroglyph that only a qualified linguist may comprehend. And that just doesn't sit right. "Any man with a vital knowledge of the human psychology," wrote G. K. Chesterton, "ought to have the most profound suspicion of anybody who claims to be an artist, and talks a great deal about art. Art is a right and human thing, like walking or saying one's prayers; but the moment it begins to be talked about very solemnly, a man may be fairly certain that the thing has come into a congestion and a kind of difficulty."

As I write, theory seems to have run its course. Cultural studies—the latest version of humanism—flourishes, but it is doubtful that the *New York Times Magazine* will be plucking any new literature professors from the academy and featuring them in its pages any time soon. Nonetheless, theory has taken its toll on the general culture. By emphatically denying the aesthetic or transcendent qualities of literature, by calling into question intentionality and design, by squeezing the elusive symmetry of poetry into semiotic form, the theorists have lumped art with philosophy. And by holding literature accountable to the values inherent in a particular culture, the materialists have managed to confuse society with humanity. Like it or not, the way students of literature think about novels and poems has been altered: Stephen King is taught alongside Henry James; Rita Dove appears on a syllabus with Robert Frost; King Lear and King Kong are spoken of in the same breath. No more do critics refer to the transformative powers of art; no longer do they regard the sublime and the transcendent as part of their mandate. That was in another country, and, besides, those writers are dead.

Where, one wonders, do we go from here? If "the socioeconomic conditions of the classic act of reading no longer obtain," as George Steiner argues, "or obtain only in the artifice of the academic," what then is the future of literature? It is safe only to say that the pendulum's motion continues, and that what is considered today the proper avenue to teach literature will be closed for repairs tomorrow. There may indeed be no universal truth regarding the way people respond to books; still, it may be confidently said that art is not foremost in the business of rectifying injustice or inequality, it is not about the suffering masses. It is about those who are born with a need and a gift to create, and about people whose nature and intelligence compel them to seek and understand such creation.

We must decide for ourselves whether art is defined entirely by context or whether—because of some essential and unfathomable quality—it transcends the artist and the age that produced it.

Depending on one's inclinations, one will think either like a theorist or like an artist. Although certain books endure because they are admired and loved by a large segment of the public, they were conceived in private by individuals who, because of the books *they* had read, recognized that the rules of the game had changed when it came to a certain kind of writing. Literature (like painting, sculpture, music, and architecture) is conversation among artists, and if one is not aided by temperament or education to overhear that dialogue, many works of art must remain mute. And there is no shame in this. The appreciation of literature is not a given: not everyone is meant to be a serious reader or writer, or to appreciate, to the same degree, the original, clever, wonderful, or sneaky arrangement of words that suddenly hit just the right note, shake loose previously held beliefs, explode old meanings, create a new authority, and just make you glad to be reading.

In the end, art is all too human—which is to say, it is personal. This is not to say, however, as so many commentators insist on doing, that art celebrates life; it may or may not depending on the artist's motives for getting down to work. Rather, art, if it deserves the name, always celebrates art. And that is the reason that no institution—not the academy or committees or government-sponsored programs—can ever define or produce it. Hence, the reclamation of literature from academic purists is not something that should concern us unduly. Literature depends on literature to emerge, and as long as there are writers who familiarize themselves with tradition, master their craft, and begin afresh, the prose and poetry that we cannot predict and do not expect will continue to find their way to us.

[1992]

12

How We Write When We
Write About Writing

—————

Near the beginning of *Enemies of Promise,* that strange alloy of literary criticism and autobiography, Cyril Connolly contends that "it should be possible to learn as much about an author's income and sex-life from one paragraph of his writing as from his cheque stubs and his love letters." Though this is probably more of a conceit than firm conviction (one can barely identify a writer's sex, much less sex life, from what may be a few impersonal sentences), Connolly was expressing a general confidence in style's transparency. "It is most true, *stylus virum arguit,* our style betrays us," wrote Robert Burton—a thought later immortalized in Buffon's: *"Le style est l'homme même."*

It is, of course, far easier to point out style's effects than to define its essential quality. Connolly proposes that literary style is roughly divisible into the Mandarin and the Vernacular. The former, served up by Sir Thomas Browne, Addison, Dr. Johnson, Gibbon, Ruskin, Pater, Wilde, and Henry James, rejoices in complexity, eloquence, and subtlety, unfurling them in one dependent clause after another. The Vernacular is a less formal affair, whose practitioners—Hazlitt, Butler, Shaw, Wells, Gissing, Orwell, and Maugham—draw on patterns of ordinary speech and the brisk rhythms of journalism. The line separating the two styles, however, is a fluid one. There is "a relationship between them," Connolly observes, "a perpetual action and reaction," which began with the rise of Fleet Street and the founding of the literary *Reviews* toward the end of the eighteenth century.

Connolly's own thoughts on style were expressed a few short years before World War II. Since then much has changed in the way literary criticism is regarded and practiced both here and abroad. In fact, the change has been so drastic that Geoffrey Hartman, the Karl Young Professor of English and Comparative Literature at Yale, is within his rights to subsume the Mandarin and the Vernacular under one rubric, variously called the Familiar-, the Conversational-, or, rather cloyingly, the Friendship-Style. Now competing with the old lettristic style is the theoretical or academic style, defined by Hartman as "prose with a noticeable proportion of technical terms." Of course, Hartman means much more by this than an infusion of mouthy words, and though there is little that is stylish about theoretical discourse, it *is* a style, for only as a style can it have the broad and deep cultural implications he ascribes to it.

Hartman, who has written elsewhere on detective fiction and the movies, as well as on subjects befitting his position, has given his book *Minor Prophecies* the subtitle *The Literary Essay in the Culture Wars* because, despite its other concerns, this is a book about the tension between the two kinds of critical style. And though Hartman goes out of his way to assure us that this tension, like that between the Mandarin and the Vernacular, is beneficial, and that both styles have their uses, and that the contemporary polemic about the two styles is really "the product of a misunderstanding," just about everything he says regarding theory's emergence speaks for its superiority.

Committed to a point of view, but not to a sustained argument, the book's ten chapters explore differences between Anglo-American and Continental criticism, the origins of the review-essay, the politics of literary restitution, and the place of F. R. Leavis and Paul de Man, among others, in the intellectual pantheon. But because this is first and foremost a book about critical prose and the status of the essay as "a reflective and clarifying genre," one may perhaps compress and restructure the broken, underlying argument into a three-tiered thesis, although not without the inevitable loss in nuance and complexity: (1) All forms of writing designate a relationship between writer and public; between the written word and the world it signifies. (2) By implication, then, style demonstrates both the ability and willingness to comprehend and participate in a worldview that is successive and grounded in history. (3) And by extension, style embodies the increasing self-consciousness that history has forced upon us—a process, which, if understood, may have both a practical and transcendent dimension.

To put it in even blunter terms: Because the theoretical style has established itself in the world of letters, there must be valid reasons for its success. The generative cause, for Hartman, is to be found in the emotional reaction to World War I. Citing Valéry's comment that "something deeper has been worn away than the renewable parts of the machine . . . our fears are infinitely more precise than our hopes," he suggests that the disturbed balance of hope and dread has informed our thinking about the world and the word. How much more this balance was affected by the horrors of the next world war remains, of course, unquantifiable. But this mournful assessment of history is today almost certainly taken for granted. Francis Fukuyama, for example, begins *The End of History and the Last Man* by claiming: "The twentieth century, it is safe to say, has made all of us into deep historical pessimists."

Such pessimism not only clouds the future but also permeates the physical and philosophical present. A loss of faith in the capacity to know either ourselves or nature in any absolute sense distinguishes us from the generations born before 1900. Matter, or the atoms that constitute it, can be neither defined nor measured without allowing for statistical probabilities. And words, as Saussure and his church of latter-day signifiers continue to preach, have no referents. Thinking about thinking has taken a strange, impersonal turn—as has thinking about literature. The analytic displacement of German philosophy and its explicit concern with subjective intentionality (which later turns up in phenomenology and existentialism) by schools of thought that examine the unconscious representations of self and society embodied in our artifacts, especially language, has made, as everyone will agree, a deep impression on literary criticism. Instead of wrestling with manifestations of individual genius or will, theory-minded critics—structuralists, semioticians, and deconstructionists—emphasize the linguistic properties of prose, exposing the unconscious interplay between social and semiotic structures.

In effect, Hartman offers us a historical brief for the critical style that goes by the name of theory. The decorum of the conversational style was fine when we knew less and hoped for more, but it is unrepresentative of the postmodern perspective. Indeed, its civility, wit, temperateness, and unmediated belief in the civilizing influence of art may actually be inappropriate in light of the barbarism that haunts the twentieth century—the barbarism that prompted Adorno's injunction regarding the writing of poetry after Auschwitz.

That a certain ineffectuality exists where *belles lettres* meets science or politics is, I think, unarguable. But is theoretical criticism any more equal to the task? Hartman believes it to be, but his justification subtly begs the question; one cannot demonstrate an idea's or an event's inalienable rightness by adducing everything that preceded it. History happens and makes things happen, but what conclusions can we draw regarding a thing's historical appositeness? Yes, the Great War shocked artists and intellectuals; and yes, Wittgenstein, Saussure, the Vienna Circle, the Frankfurt School, psychoanalysis, Heidegger, World War II, structuralism, deconstruction, hermeneutical theory, not to mention the French radicals' demand for a new language to replace the nasty old values implicit in bourgeois discourse, all had their effects on literature. The question that needs asking, however, is whether such effects are significant in any but a temporal sense; how much weight does being representative of the times carry? For Hartman, the issue is plain. Intellectual history has tossed up literary theory, and so, despite the benefits supposedly to be gained from the tension between the theoretical and the conversational style, Hartman has no qualms about declaring that the "gain of literary theory in the 1970s was a gain in thoughtfulness."

Which brings us to the second point, concerning the intellectual endowment of the two styles. Is there, as Hartman suggests, a sense of things accessible to one style but not to another? Furthermore, should what "is important in art be translatable into terms of colloquial prose, or does the effort coopt the work of genius, repressing its asocial or antisocial component? And, again, does the insistence that criticism imitate the seeming clarity of public speech neglect the creativeness of critical prose itself, both as a technique of discovery and a style developed over time?"

Although such questions suggest a willingness at least to consider the limitations of the theoretical style, only someone who firmly hews to the greater efficacy of the theoretical over the conversational could approve of the following exegetical model:

> The necessary, originary, and irreducible dissimulation of the meaning of being, its occultation within the very blossoming forth of presence, that retreat without which there would be no history of being which was completely *history* and history of

being, Heidegger's insistence on noting that being is produced as history only through the logos, and is nothing outside of it, the difference between being and the entity—all this clearly indicates that fundamentally nothing escapes the movement of the signifier and that, in the last instance, the difference between signified and signifier is *nothing*. (Derrida, *Of Grammatology*)

Or could himself write:

Yet theory too is often associated by us with the contrary of a critical position, with a systematic or ideological closure that appropriates one part of existence, or of language, at the expense of others. Theory is then accused of forgetting its own positivity, that it is not nature, that no neutral totality exists, and that totalization should be in the service of a critical or comparative counter-perspective. Indeed, totalization, and its most obvious figure, prolepsis, cannot be avoided, because we are always situated. The domain of preunderstanding (what we have always already known) coheres us, makes understanding, in all its error, possible, makes dialogue and agreement possible.

A good many readers may be excused for thinking this is all flapdoodle, but it is also necessary to say that many intelligent men and women, mostly academics to be sure, will feel perfectly at home with these sentences. For such readers, the problematic nature of both mind and language requires a style that is emblematic of such difficulty. This being the case, any attempt to review a book of theory in the conversational style may itself be only a futile gesture in translation. Still, one bravely pushes on.

In fact, cautions Hartman, the critic who relies on the conversational style "because of its propriety may actually be doing a disservice to language [so much for his professed acceptance of this style]. However difficult Blackmur, Burke, Heidegger, or Derrida may be, there is less entropy in them than in those who translate with the best intentions hazardous ideas or expressions into ordinary speech." Apparently, hazardous ideas, presumably those we may find disconcerting, lie outside the scope of ordinary, as opposed to theoretical, discourse; and ultimately the deeper meaning of texts can be rendered only in a technical metalanguage. The unstated correlation is with particle physics, which requires a language of symbols and mathematical equations to express newly discovered relations among mass, energy, and the observer.

Some remarks by Paul Ricoeur may prove instructive here. After noting that scientific language, by aspiring to the ideal representation of nature, is contextually neutral (since its truth is *already* the truth of what is being described), Ricoeur argues that ordinary language "differs from an ideal language in that it has no fixed expressions independent of their contextual uses . . . the interpretative process as it occurs in the use of ordinary language foreshadows the more difficult, evasive, and complicated interpretation of texts." In other words, it is precisely because "there is something irreducible in ordinary language" that we are able to communicate and interpret communication legitimately.

To take this further, even theoretical language is, at bottom, ordinary. Try as they might, literary theorists cannot earn scientific accreditation; all that the theorist can do is pull and stretch ordinary language to make it accommodate abstruse philosophical concepts. Needless to say, the language of philosophers, with one or two exceptions, has been tough sledding ever since Aristotle decided to get technical; and it is a thorny issue indeed whether its difficulty is essential to, or commensurate with, the difficulty of its ideas. Much the same thing, of course, can be said about literary theory. Are there really thoughts not only too deep for tears but also for the familiar vocabulary?

Difficult to say. Language, after all, not only expresses thoughts but also makes possible thoughts that could not exist without it. Just how it accomplishes this or what role esoteric words play are issues still in need of clarification. Nevertheless, an uncomplicated style does not necessarily reduce texts to uncomplicated ideas. But what the conversational style does avoid is the cognitive quagmire that all epistemological questions ultimately sink into. The idea of the duality between subject and object, between the truth of a thing and knowing the thing, puts philosophical language through some amazing loops, circumvolutions that attest to the impossibility of absolute answers.

Hartman is not unmindful of the problem. He mentions repeatedly the "impasse" created by deconstructionist theory and concedes willingly enough the "methodological pathos" at the heart of deconstruction, "a mourning over the self-invalidating nature of all methodologies." Still, one cannot help feeling that he would rather mourn than not know enough to mourn.

To his credit, he does not condone difficulty for its own sake. He believes that the problematic nature of interpretation and the self-referential process of thinking have fashioned a style whose difficulty is suggestive of the greater problems it deals with. Clarity is hardly the point. And while Hartman would, I think, frown on those who maintain that clarity, being part of a bourgeois value system, is another form of oppression, he might agree that clarity has been overrated—an opinion that unfortunately has found a home in the academy.

Which brings us to Hartman's third point: the place of theory in contemporary culture. It seems that our need for theory is "linked to a change in the environment: the rise of propaganda, organized lying and ideological falsification." Evidently, it is in theory's power to see through and disclose our spiritual failings. Likening this unmasking capability to Talmudic commentary, Hartman muses that: "We have something to learn from a religious culture in which the creative energies went almost totally into commentary, and the same basic method of reading was used for law (halakhah) and lore (aggadah)."

But whatever his hopes for literary theory, Hartman never quite demonstrates just how this interpretative process leads to the realization that a "critical essay, a legal opinion, an interpretation of Scripture, a biography, can be as inspiring and nurturing as poem, novel, or painting." Rather, it is all too evident that theory's involvement with a text is really a means to get more intimately involved with itself, and to stake out a position independent of literary sources.

Theory reigns. Not in the literary reviews or in the general press, but certainly in the majority of books issuing from university presses and in many graduate schools from Yale to Berkeley. And up to a point, readers who take literature seriously must familiarize themselves with the works of Adorno, Benjamin, Lukács, Barthes, Derrida, Paul de Man, and another half-dozen or so philosopher-critics whose works have affected the way literature is taught.

But such an acknowledgment is a far cry from avowing that the entire panoply of twentieth-century intellectual thought justifies theory's eminence in contemporary literature departments. There are, after all, less exalted reasons for this phenomenon, including the conspicuous absence in the last quarter century of writers of genius, a fact that may have something to do with how critics regard their own labors. Nor can we dismiss the allure that a professional insularity has for some teachers and critics. Once it became clear that the shift from *belles lettres* to literary specialization was a going concern, and that a familiarity with what might be considered more analytical disciplines—philosophy, linguistics, anthropology—was essential to advancement, many English professors took to the theoretical style and never looked back. In a word, clarity was no longer a good career move.

Like it or not, one must admit that Hartman argues from

strength: literary theory has exploded myths and assumptions about meaning and intentionality, rushing past the poetic source to grapple with the mental categories that determine how we create and receive verbal information. And what is implicit in theory's program (a point that Hartman avoids) is its demotion of individual talent. The emphasis on common semiotic structures in all forms of discourse is what, after all, brought about the death of the author and the current skepticism concerning the usefulness of "quality" and "beauty." Indeed, the technical jargon and impersonal tone of the theoretical style perfectly mirror an age in which individuality in art is no longer prized.

Will this style prevail? That depends, I think, not so much on historical forces as on a human need for harmony and certitude. "Our language," remarked Cyril Connolly, "is a sulky and inconstant beauty and at any given moment it is important to know what liberties she will permit." Few academic critics today seem aware of the existence of the proprieties: the only style that is intellectually appropriate is one that demonstrates just how involuted, uncertain, fragmentary, and perpetually in flux the process of thinking is.

Agreed, there are good reasons not to cease from mental fight. Metaphysical and linguistic questions need to be pondered, however inconclusive our speculations prove to be. But we may also ask ourselves whether such deliberations can be profitably turned to the study of literature. There is something about art that resists theory, just as there is something about existence that defies unbiased or conclusive judgments. To do art, one must cease from philosophizing; to offer criticism of art, one must walk a fine line between art and philosophy, never leaning too far in either direction.

A man who knew something about theory once described philosophy as thinking that reveals that the simple is complicated, that doubts may reside in firmly held convictions, and that even the most plausible premises are vulnerable to logical attack. "The net result of these speculations," added Bertrand Russell, "is to substitute articulate hesitation for inarticulate certainty." Without wishing either to detract from speculative thought or insist on a simplistic and apodictic universe, one may choose, where literature is concerned, a little less articulate hesitation, a little more inarticulate certainty. Without this faith in things and words, neither art nor criticism can truly matter to us.

[1992]

13

Looking for a Good Argument:
Argument and the Novel

I s argument returning to the novel? I don't mean generational feuds or emotional scuffling between the sexes but argument with some metaphysical meat on its bones. In the past several years, novels by Cynthia Ozick, Umberto Eco, and the late John Gardner have unabashedly pondered what Lionel Trilling called "the great issues with which the mind has traditionally been concerned: whence and whither, birth and death, fate, free will, and immortality." Trilling felt that in neglecting these issues, mid-twentieth-century fiction had suffered a loss of emotional power. This may be putting the case too strongly; impassioned dialogue about ideas, however, has not exactly been a staple of the contemporary novel.

One immediately thinks of exceptions—the philosophically inclined novels of Iris Murdoch and John Fowles, the fabulistic tales of Stanislaw Lem and Italo Calvino, the politically allusive work of Milan Kundera and Mario Vargas Llosa, the metaphysical fictions of Jorge Luis Borges. Closer to home, Philip Roth's writer about town, Nathan Zuckerman, justifies the ways of Zuckerman

to Jews, while Saul Bellow's brainy heroes shoot various intellectual rapids.

All the same, good argument is hard to find. I mean the
framing of antithetical world views, presented by fictional characters whose behavior evolves from these views. The split can take
various forms—intellect versus faith, idealism versus materialism,
Hellenism versus Hebraism, free will versus predestination, nature
versus nurture, nihilism versus meaning or value, and so forth.
Characters may muse on these issues, debate them with others,
talk ostensibly about one thing while meaning something else, but
in each case the discussion must be managed so that we believe, if
not in the character's point of view, then at least in the conviction
with which it is put forward.

Every genuine novel implicitly argues its relation to the world,
the debate in the text being only one of several narrative devices at
the writer's disposal. Ideas don't have to be ventilated by cerebral
characters to be present, and novels without polemics (think of
Heart of Darkness, To the Lighthouse, or *Lord of the Flies*) aren't
necessarily less rewarding or profound than those that effusively
toss ideas around. Yet I confess to reading novels mainly for the
talk they contain—not only for the nuanced, gritty, or eloquent talk
we associate with various walks of life but for the sermons, tirades,
and arguments about those great issues. I relish arguments about
the nature of God and man. I enjoy having my opinions challenged
or affirmed by characters whose intelligence I respect. What's
more, I still entertain faint hopes that somewhere in the thrashing
out of issues lies a clue to the existential riddles that taunt me.

Argument in literature, of course, did not originate with novels, but harks back to the Greeks. Homer's gods bickered, Achilles
and Agamemnon quarreled, Antigone set herself against Creon,
and in the *Oresteia* Athena and Apollo debated whether it is
worse to murder one's mother or one's father. What may seem like
hairsplitting was, in fact, argument that touched on the social fab-

ric; more was involved here than ordinary litigation. All serious argument is ethical, elucidating man's relation to God and society, and the implications can be startling. What could be more audacious than that first argument presented by Job to God? Muriel Spark's novel *The Only Problem* puts it in a nutshell: Job "not only argued the problem of suffering, he suffered the problem of argument. And that is incurable."

Incurable or no, how a culture treats the problem of argument illustrates its openness, its willingness to doubt. At the risk of oversimplification, one might say that argument in the Middle Ages was confined to the interpretation of irrefutable religious truths; beyond a certain point it became heresy. Hence the priggish abbot in Umberto Eco's *Name of the Rose* quite properly warns the monks not to "give way . . . to the pleasure of disputation." Two centuries later, however, a Renaissance man like Montaigne could comfortably admit entering "into discussion with great freedom and ease. . . . No propositions astonish me, no belief offends me, whatever contrast it offers with my own."

Although the evolving relation between belief and discourse is difficult to trace, we find evidence of it in literature. With the novel, however, the task is complex, because as a late-blooming genre, it was an outgrowth of earlier literary traditions and the cultural forces prevalent during the eighteenth century. One such force was a philosophical commitment to subjectivity, the project of extracting ideas from their Platonic casings and grounding them, as it were, in human nature. Rendered "human," such general notions as progress, science, imagination, spirit, and knowledge became more problematic than ever—but also splendid material for novelists, who recognized that ideas shape character as much as character illustrates ideas. Try imagining Julien Sorel in *The Red and the Black* minus his infatuation with Napoleon (whom Hegel had called "an idea on horseback") or Levin in *Anna Karenina* without the idea of land reform, or practically any major character in a

Dostoevsky novel without a devout or adversarial relation to God. When called on, Jane Austen's heroines also give a good accounting of themselves—witness Catherine Morland in *Northanger Abbey* in an argument about the writing of history: "the men all so good for nothing, and hardly any women at all."

One of the more intellectually weighted arguments in novels occurs in Thomas Mann's *Magic Mountain*. The Jesuit-trained nihilist Naphta and the progressive liberal atheist Settembrini lock horns over man's destiny. One embraces the primitive in human nature, the desire for mystery, war, and a vengeful God. The other exalts compassion and reason. Though not subtly argued, these different positions are laid out with great care and without self-consciousness. I say this because by 1924, the year Mann's book was published, the novel of ideas was already something of a literary dinosaur, seeming too bulky and primitive for the new environment of modernism. In fact, as early as 1907, E. M. Forster's *Longest Journey* had betrayed a disenchantment with abstractions. Although Forster's novel opens with a typical undergraduate argument about the reality of objects, specifically that of a cow, the emphasis is decidedly empirical: The cow "seemed to make things easier. She was so familiar, so solid, that surely the truths that she illustrated would in time become familiar and solid also. Is the cow there or not? This was better than deciding between objectivity and subjectivity."

Reaffirming British philosophy's empirical cast, Forster's bias was also a prescient one. Developments in particle physics over the next quarter-century would argue for the statistical inclusion of chance and an "uncertainty relation" in the workings of nature, as well as the absence of a privileged position from which to observe reality. I don't wish to labor the correlation between scientific, philosophic, and esthetic approaches to truth, but surely this disruption of classical mechanics influenced the operations of artists and philosophers. A case in point is the philosophers of the

Vienna Circle, who discarded psychologism and idealism in favor of a verifiability principle. The business of philosophy, they insisted, was not to speculate on matters impossible to confirm but to analyze sense data and to analyze this analysis—with the result that the only reality language seemed capable of conveying was the reality of language. Everything else was guesswork.

But what of novelists? Could they also legitimately dispense with ideas while continuing to bring us news about the world—the novel's traditional function? In a way, years before philosophers frowned on metaphysics, novelists were given the green light from the Master himself. In her short book *Ideas and the Novel,* Mary McCarthy says flatly that Henry James "etherealized the novel . . . and perhaps etherized it as well. . . . With James, the novel renounced its actuality, its power to move masses . . . it no longer had any need for ideas." For McCarthy, the novel as fine art is at variance with the novel of ideas, and to a large degree this is true, for when life is consecrated to the ideal of art, ideas lose something of their human character, their connection to the perturbations of the mind and spirit that engender them. James, of course, is full of ideas. It is only the misconception that he is the exemplary novelist without ideas that has encouraged his literary heirs to promote nuance and inflection over churning plots and polemics. Ironically, the legacy of James's textured, many-layered prose is the minimalist style of an Ann Beattie or a Raymond Carver, who bring us the deep resonances found in small noises.

Viewing the decline of argument in novels from another angle, one finds that with the end of World War I, the few grand ideas of the preceding century had either dissipated or been split and appropriated by warring factions. In philosophy this meant increasingly technical disputes about language, while in politics ideas became equated with ideological positions—Communism,

socialism, Fascism, Stalinism, Trotskyism. For the novel to have
successfully rendered these proliferating beliefs, a Balzac or Dostoevsky would have been necessary, and that would have gone
against the modernist grain. Indeed, modernism has not been kind
to the novel, which by midcentury had been eclipsed by the plastic
arts and film as the esthetic conduit of choice.

I don't mean to suggest that ideas were summarily expelled
from fiction around 1925, only that absolutes in general had become suspect, and since argument presupposes that universal
ideas are not only authentic but also relevant to our lives, it too was
seen to serve no useful function in novels. By the 1960s canonical
nineteenth-century interpretations of life or texts had become unfashionable, and the division between high and low culture and
that between fact and fiction was often blurred. Truman Capote
wrote a factual account of a crime that seemed more fictional than
many novels, and the same might be said of Tom Wolfe's report-
ing. What was important was to get at the immediacy of experience, to cut through the philosophical vapors and reveal the visible
in all its hectic manifestations. Those great but invisible issues
mourned by Trilling had died a natural—that is to say, historical—
death, and for some critics the novel died with them.

In fact, by the time I began to read serious fiction around 1965,
the novel had already been "moribund" for fifteen or so years, and
writers like Alain Robbe-Grillet and Nathalie Sarraute were fashioning "new novels" that purported to demonstrate the obsoles-
cence of plot, character, and metaphor. But this was also a time
when Saul Bellow, Gabriel García Márquez, Aleksandr Solzheni-
tsyn, and Bernard Malamud were just hitting their stride. In 1965
the novel wasn't any less vital than in 1925 or 1900, but it was
different. Fewer characters were gripped by doctrinal ideas, yet
more seemed entangled in questions of race, sex, and ethnicity.
Philosophical argument was indeed missing, but that was to be

expected if novels, as Trilling himself noted, reflect "a culture's hum and buzz of implication."

The questions are whether the hum and buzz has taken on a deeper tone and whether that indicates a greater receptivity to ideas. I think it has and does. Certainly the need for meaning is central to Cynthia Ozick's novel *The Cannibal Galaxy,* which pits Joseph Brill, educator, against Hester Lilt, philosopher. Titles aside, Ozick means for us to see them as two fundamentally opposed intelligences. For Brill "the cosmos was always inhuman, of a terrible coldness, and far away, even though one lived in its midst." For Hester Lilt "it was a long finger tapping." Without advancing a specific doctrine, Hester sounds at times like a gnostic Aristotle, guaranteeing the universal by virtue of the particular, positing nature as a series of graded existences leading to the one Existence that vouchsafes the others. Brill thinks he knows better. He's stuck in the shifting, indeterminate sublunar world from which he derives his sly and skeptical outlook.

When they finally collide over the question of Hester's daughter's intelligence, what emerges is a struggle between the concepts of existence and essence. There is a certain effrontery in this—I mean, in Ozick's indifference to the familiar or the sensational. But to say she is irredeemably intellectual is unfair, for whenever she pits the mercurial intelligence of Brill against the impassive intelligence of Lilt, she gives life to mind, distilling from abstraction its human elements.

Intelligence carries with it an obligation—it must be put to use. This point is forcefully brought home in John Gardner's last novel, *Mickelsson's Ghosts.* Rarely has so much argument—good and bad, reasonable and preposterous—found its way into recent fiction. Mickelsson, a large, boozing, hamfisted professor of moral philosophy, goes on frequent intellectual binges, taking on every topic under the sun, conjuring up priests and psychiatrists to debate with when no one else is available, or invoking the great thinkers of the past, often on flimsy pretexts—and for what? Argument doesn't prevent his life from collapsing around him, but it does keep him honest. Nothing gets by him, especially not his own foolishness. In short, Mickelsson's excited, suffering intelligence never loses sight of the fact that thinking is moral, which is why fundamentalism—"a secure closing of doors, permission not to think"—ultimately is immoral.

Although reviewers generally seemed more comfortable dealing with these novels on a stylistic level, the books' salient feature is a frank espousal of ideas, put across in argument form. Whether this augurs a revival of argument in novels probably depends more on the exigencies of the marketplace than on novelists' interest in ideas. A promising sign, however, of the public's willingness to attend closely to philosophical discussion is the success of *The Name of the Rose*, in which a series of grisly murders seems merely an excuse for arguments about some of Christianity's finer points.

In any event, arguments will never cease—not because people will always disagree but because they will continue to think. "It is the nature of thought to be indefinite," Coleridge once remarked. So it is. The indefiniteness arises from the melancholy fact that thought can never impartially examine itself; whatever we decide about the universe and our place in it, some degree of uncertainty will remain. For every answer, there will be the possibility of an equal and opposite answer. The best illustration of this concerns the dialectic between speech and the unknowable. There is Wittgenstein's oft-quoted remark: "Whereof one cannot speak, thereon one must be silent." This seems right. But there is also Nietzsche's observation: "It seems to me that even the bluntest word, the bluntest letter, is still more good-natured than silence. . . . All who remain silent are dyspeptic." That seems right too.

[1985]

14

Just Imagine:
Three Hundred Years of the Creative Imagination

anguage, an entomological etymologist might say, is a
hive of activity, aswarm in competing fictions. Words fly
in and out of the mind, and the hum and buzz of implication rises and subsides as the world grows older. New
words are coined, old words are lost, others survive only at the
expense of their former authority. "Taste" for example, or "temperament"—words that once summoned a complicated set of notions about the world and human nature—retain today only an
echo of the intellectual resonance that other centuries took for
granted. Another case in point—one that may surprise—is "imagination." True, it is still a good old-fashioned word, handy and
reliable, yet no great seriousness attaches itself to its use. We
bother neither to define nor to explain it, but allow almost reflex-
ively that it is what contemporary poets and statesmen want more
of. And its purpose, which was once of such profound relevance
to artists, writers, and philosophers, has mostly vanished. The
proof? The proof is that it requires an act of deep imagining to
appreciate the station it once had in the intellectual universe.

Two hundred years ago, the imagination meant *something;* to

some it meant nearly *everything*. If you do not believe me, please
refer to James Engell's *The Creative Imagination,* a robust and
thorough examination of the word's origins, its philosophical underpinnings, and the astonishing expectations it fostered in the
hundred years between the middle of the eighteenth century and
the middle of the nineteenth. From 1740 to 1820 the idea of the
imagination was anatomized and reconstructed, bisected and tri-
sected, embroidered and inflated, and variously offered up as
a panacea for all human and metaphysical ills, as the summum
bonum of mankind, as the one true path to God, nature, and
art. The imagination, so Engell declaims, replaced the Platonic-
Aristotelian world order, formed "a hinge connecting the Enlightenment and Romanticism," and in effect "introduce[d] the modern era." Now whether the imagination had quite the vast and
demonstrable influence Engell claims for it is arguable: what is not
debatable, however, is the tremendous interest it generated. Surely
there have not been many subjects about which so much has been
written by so many in so short a time.

The intellectual bustle around the question of the imagination
toward the latter part of the eighteenth century was, of course,
inseparable from the philosophical fervor that swept the European
capitals of learning. A farrago of epistemological, philological, social, and religious strategies flourished contemporaneously, often
setting off and sometimes obscuring one another. An abbreviated
list might include: Cartesianism, Berkeleian idealism, Lockean empiricism, and Humean skepticism (which laid the foundations for
empirical psychology and associationism); the obsessions with
Hellenism and the Orient; pietism; the apotheosis of Newton for
having mechanized the universe; the propagation of *Volkspoesie,*
individualism, and nationalism; the concern with progress, as well
as with its repudiation—all of which attested to the final sloughing
off of Renaissance and neoclassical beliefs.

The problem, then, in tracing the history of an idea through these interweaving schemes and meditations is knowing where to begin. Engell begins with the "new philosophy [that] calls all in doubt." For Donne and his generation, the Copernican revolution had produced a world "all in peeces, all cohaerence gone." To counteract this uncertainty and reestablish what could not be doubted, Descartes embraced a methodology based on mathematics, but which ultimately rested on an intuitive syllogism. And in formulating an apodictic epistemology, Descartes also presumed a dualism of thought and extension that would thereafter haunt both idealists and rationalists unwilling to admit division in "real" knowledge.

To contain the dualism, Enlightenment philosophers envisioned the world as a single system whose orderly and immutable laws could be derived empirically and properly applied to human affairs. The same reason that guided Descartes and Newton could thus validate the social sciences, psychology, and religion. But reason, it seemed, could also be used against itself. Strict empiricists reasoned that axiomatic, universally valid laws could not be logically demonstrated. For Locke, knowledge was at best an "association of ideas"; and Hume, a half century later, argued that causality was a psychological phenomenon, an expression of the "vivacity of our ideas." This emphasis on the connection of ideas as the matrix for both particulars and universals was later parlayed by the associationists into a sensibility overseen by the imagination.

Nor did complete faith in reason meet with the universal approval of less empirically minded thinkers. The cognitive laws debunked by Hume were also anathema to the pietists, for whom truth existed only in the emotion of genuine spiritual experience. Thus both the skeptic and the pietist—one by using logic to limit its own powers, the other by dismissing that power entirely—eased the entry of the imagination into mental life.

This was the situation confronting Kant when he set out to show how the mind could make synthetic a priori judgments about sense data that were necessarily valid. The dualism that lay at the core of any empirical epistemology had to be, if not logically expunged, then creatively joined in the mind, where the imagination was already waiting to take a role, though perhaps not as central a role as stipulated by Engell. Integral to all this theorizing about the fallibility and infallibility of reason was the idea that the mind was both an active and passive participant where knowledge was concerned—a view subliminally reflected in the division of the imagination into the plastic and the imitative.

All this has to be sketched in, as Engell does, before one can grasp the place assigned to the imagination during the late Enlightenment when, Engell notes, a man of learning in one thing was a man of learning in all things, when there existed among the disciplines (and among nations) what Samuel Johnson likened to "a community of mind." So if the imagination fascinated an eighteenth-century English critic, his writings would likely be reviewed by a Scottish psychologist, a German poet, a French architect.

To be sure, the imagination was not exactly neglected before the eighteenth century. As the *nuntius* (messenger) in faculty psychology's theory of mind, the imagination mediated between sensation and judgment and could, if affected by strong stimuli, throw reason into a tizzy. Treated deferentially by such Renaissance philosophers as Montaigne and Bacon, it alarmed Burton and even elicited a cautionary warning from Spenser, who urged poets not to make a "monster of their fantasie." This wariness was later taken up by Dr. Johnson, who observed that were it not for the imagination, a man would be as happy in the arms of a chambermaid as in those of a duchess.

On a less visceral level, the imagination retained its Aristotelian meaning of "thinking with images." But neither the emotional nor visual connotation suggested the potent and meliorative powers the imagination would assume during the Enlightenment, when it became, in Engell's phrase, "a human reflex of God's creative energy." As such, it contained and explained "sympathy," "genius," "originality," and "poetry." It extended man's knowledge of the world, not by dismissing or overriding reason, but by enhancing it. By 1786, Sir Joshua Reynolds was only one of many who saw the imagination as "the residence of truth."

Engel's accomplishment, for which we ought to be grateful, is to disabuse us forever of the notion that the imagination was a Romantic invention or that its original function was connected with poetics. The fact is, before the turn of the eighteenth century, the imagination was mainly deployed in a philosophical, psychological, or social capacity—a point brought home by Engell's discussions of Hobbes, Locke, Hume, Johnson; Bodmer, Wolff, Platner, Kant, Hamann; and the English and Scottish associationists: David Hartley, William Duff, Dugald Steward, James Arbuckle, Francis Hutcheson, James Beattie, Archibald Alison, and Abraham Tucker.

Of those early works that deal with the imagination as a potential critical tool, Engell scans Shaftesbury's *Characteristics of Men, Manners, Opinions, Times* (1711), Akenside's *Pleasures of the Imagination* (1744), Edward Young's *Conjectures on Original Composition* (1759), Lord Kames's *Elements of Criticism* (1762), Lord Monboddo's *Of the Origin and Progress of Language* (1773), and Alexander Gerard's *Essay on Genius* (1774)—works that enabled the imagination to become "the first artery joining philosophy and psychology with the arts and criticism." Eventually, these sundry ruminations would be collected by the English Romantics (Hazlitt, Coleridge, Wordsworth) and by the *Sturm und Drang* poets (Schiller, Goethe) and applied categorically to the arts.

As for the presumed dichotomy between reason and imagination, it was not a concept favored by Romantic poets, who saw poetry as a valid conduit of knowledge. Shelley's cognitive claims for the creative faculty as "the basis of all knowledge" echoed the imagination's importance in Kantian architectonics as the mediating faculty between sense and understanding, without which the mind could not reproduce temporal order or conceive distinct objects. In short, the imagination was not regarded by most Romantics as simply an instrument that could mold the "spontaneous overflow of emotions recollected in tranquility" into poetry. Instead, it represented for them that power of the mind which could successfully integrate the concepts of God, man, and nature into a harmonious whole.

Because everyone had something to say about the imagination, Engell sees connections everywhere. With evangelical fervor, he catalogues a hundred-year period of elaborate intellectual cross-pollination. Akenside borrowed from Locke and Shaftesbury. Shaftesbury, through Leibniz, "served as a velvet shoehorn for the revival of Spinoza, and later influenced Herder, Kant, and Schiller." Kant's construct of the transcendental imagination drew on the work of Wolff, Gerard, Sulzer, and Tetens. Hazlitt's ideas about the sympathetic imagination (a hairsbreadth from Keats's negative capability) was derived from Hume, Gerard, Priestley, Beattie, and Tucker. Coleridge dipped into everyone's work and his famous distinction between fancy and imagination recalls Dryden, Addison, Akenside, and Johnson. After a while this meticulous genealogy, with its refinements and reincarnations, becomes, to put it gently, a bit busy.

But Engell presses on, and when he says, as he does often with only the names changing, that theories of the imagination were relayed from Gerard to Tetens to Kant, baseball enthusiasts may be reminded of the old Chicago Cubs infield with the ball being whipped around from Tinker to Evers to Chance. This is said not as criticism but by way of a warning. Engell seems to have left no English, Scottish, or German philosophical stone unturned, and his necessary abridgments are not necessarily reductive.

The very comprehensiveness of the book, in fact, makes one puzzle over its omissions, of which I note three. There is only the briefest allusion to Rousseau and nary a word about Diderot. To say that French "literature and criticism . . . did not originate or develop the idea of the imagination in the same fashion nor to the same extent as that of England, Scotland, and Germany"—while true—does not, I think, justify the neglect shown by Engell. Surely Rousseau must be considered a proponent of the imagination in his *Confessions,* and the maxims in Book IV of *Emile* are suspiciously similar to certain associationist pronouncements. Kant knew Rousseau's work intimately, as did Goethe, and Wordsworth certainly echoes him. As for Diderot, didn't he claim at one point that "the model of nature is less grand than that conceived by the poet"? Hegel, too—again considering that this is a work of such magnitude—is given short shrift. Although the imagination per se does not figure in his system (an omission that does not keep Engell from invoking Leibniz), Hegel's synthesis of Kant's critical philosophy and post-Kantian strains of idealism requires, at least implicitly, an imaginative power on the part of consciousness. But on all other fronts, Engell satisfies, indeed gluts, and often one doesn't know whether to praise him for attempting so much or upbraid him for attempting too much.

Although Engell leaves off with the Romantics and does not dwell on the imagination as a religious conduit except in the cases of Blake, Coleridge, and Schelling, its religious origins are nonetheless striking. If usually a mediator between the senses and reason, the imagination also had a distinct prophetic function, one linked directly to God. Since a higher power required a higher kind of belief, what better use could be served by our imaginative capacity? This, more or less, is what Shelley meant by striving to apprehend "the Unapprehended." And even Engell's parenthetical asides on the imagination's religious dimension should alert us to its diminished role in spiritual life today. Would it be wrong to say that theologians tend to avoid the word as though it might put us in mind of fancifulness when they mean truth? It wouldn't do, after all, to have people think they only "imagine" God or their relationship to Him. One thinker, of course, who felt no trepidation in seeking God through the imagination was Kierkegaard. Almost as if sensing the word's fading power, Kierkegaard deliberately invoked it: "What feeling, knowledge, or will a man has depends on the last resort upon what imagination he has. . . . Imagination is the possibility of all reflection, and the intensity of this medium is the possibility of the intensity of the self." Of course, one might also ask: What requires more imagination: conceiving a world with God or one without Him?

If there is a problem with Engell's study, it is one of emphasis, not fact, though in a work of intellectual history this can amount to the same thing. Engell bears down so hard on the imagination's preeminence that it puts one slightly ill at ease. Was it indeed foremost in the minds of late eighteenth-century thinkers? Ubiquity does not necessarily translate as paramount concern. What about such concepts as progress, knowledge, spirit, and the absolute? Even Engell's occasional demurrers seem perfunctory, as if he cannot credit the possibility of other doctrines competing with his own. When reading a book whose analytic emphasis is so consuming, one tends to forget that other mental faculties were also being animatedly discussed at that time, ways of thinking and designating that perhaps poached on the imagination's preserves. Consider this remark by Carlyle, for example: "If called to define Shakespeare's faculty, I should say superiority of intellect, and think I had included all in that."

That said, it is only fair to acknowledge that, despite the bewildering array of references to the imagination and Engell's exhortations on its behalf, the book never loses sight of the philosophical impetus that shaped the Enlightenment's interest in it. And if, as must be the case, the reader loses sight of most of these references, one thing remains: the realization that the imagination has only the most perfunctory role in contemporary intellectual discourse. Once called upon to reveal absolute and transcendent truths, it is now enlisted in the service of disproving (and disapproving) them. Put another way: the imagination simply could not make the journey into the twentieth century when the dismantling of absolutes became a priority of language philosophers. And inevitably the word was both traduced and reduced; the flow from the subjective interior out toward universal meaning was reversed; and "imagining" became a Walt Disney-ish facet of mind engaged in pleasant reveries and storytelling. Moreover, its rote-like application to children's drawings or eccentrically charming behavior lent the word an accommodating generality, making it as applicable to the design of a pen or blender as to a work by Vermeer or Verlaine. Say something has imagination and, presto, we embellish the dull, color the bland, and make the ordinary extraordinary. How many examples of derivative novels, outlandish buildings, quirky movies, and Dada-like paintings are validated by stressing their "imaginative component"?

Yes, the imagination does come into play when we throw off inhibitions and proscriptions, and of course it is essential to creativity in both the arts and the sciences. But if every creative effort is, in the loose sense, an act of imagining, the result of such effort is not necessarily an imaginative product. That is to say, a desire to express oneself and make something new does not automatically guarantee an original work. Indeed, all too often, those unable to differentiate between the new and the original also lack the imagination to create something that is both exceptional to the past and also part of it. But this, it should be said, does not necessarily limit the imagination to ideas or artifacts that seem extravagant or unfamiliar. Sometimes it is simply the ability to *see* which requires an imaginative eye. "The difference between the Parthenon and the World Trade Center," says the intellectually intrepid Guy Davenport, "between a French wine glass and a German beer mug, between Bach and John Philip Sousa, between Sophocles and Shakespeare, between a bicycle and a horse, though explicable by historical moment, necessity, and destiny, is before all a difference of imagination." In effect, the very thing that made them is required to appreciate them, and it is in far less abundance than one might think. To imagine the imagination in this context is to feel again the amazing charge it once carried, and to understand that it is a word whose history records the history and, some might say, the diminution of the human spirit.

[1984]

15

Going, Going, Gone:
The Place of Poetry in American Letters

———

The poet must write as the interpreter of nature and the legislator of mankind.—SAMUEL JOHNSON (1759)

Poets are the unacknowledged legislators of the world.—SHELLEY (1821)

I am my own legislator and king; there is no one above me, not even God.—RILKE (1896)

"The unacknowledged legislators of the world" describes the secret police, not the poets.—W. H. AUDEN (1962)

There is these days, for those who care to notice, a sustained lull on the poetry front. For the first time in the stormy or ambivalent relations between poet and public, neither side cares enough to woo or rebuff the other. Reviewers may take the occasional swipe at poets who have garnered an undeserved reputation, but poetry itself, or rather the vocation of poetry, is no longer regarded with suspicion. Nor do poets themselves go around behaving like Byronic misfits, taking pride in their outcast state. And this, one might be surprised to learn, is of recent cultural vintage. Fifty years ago, Randall Jarrell was able to grumble that the poet was "a condemned man for whom the State will not even buy breakfast." Today, however, we know that the State is quite happy to buy most poets a decent meal, provided that they have the right connections and fill out the proper forms.

This general air of calm aside, the poets' ranks continue to swell. Although a census cannot be taken, enough people have had their status as poets confirmed by little magazines, small presses, teaching positions, art councils, artist colonies, and foundations that one can almost feel the weight of their numbers. Almost. The fact remains that poetry's audience keeps shrinking at the same time that poets' numbers continue to multiply. The reading public may sense that more poetry is being written than ever before, but is it sufficiently interested to know who exactly is writing what? Ask the general reader for a list of contemporary poets, and you will get, at most, a half dozen names. Ask for the titles of their latest books and, odds are, the answer will be a helpless shrug. In a real sense, the poet's identity today derives from his method of working, not from the fruit of that work; poets are recognized as poets not because the public knows their verse, but because they have been officially recognized by the institutions and committees that decide on such things. In the present moment, poets have been readmitted to the court and the academy, only these august bodies now go by the name of "the foundation" or "the university."

But despite their reentry into institutions of learning, poets are not actually looked to for instruction about art or society. Furthermore, poets themselves register little dissatisfaction with a culture that is, after all, hardly inimical to the literary calling. Such mutual and benign indifference is emblematic not of the decline of letters, but of the fact that poets themselves have abdicated the intellectual office that they and we once took for granted. For nearly two millennia the poet kept pace with the scholar and natural philosopher. He explained appearances, maintained links to the past, and undertook to justify the ways of the gods (and later God) to man. And poetry itself, given its mnemonic aspect, was a handy tool for learning. One thinks of Hesiod's *Works and Days,* Virgil's *Georgics,* and Lucretius's *De rerum natura.* And, not least, poetry was part of a gentleman's education: "[W]ith the exception of goodness," noted Baldesar Castiglione in the *Book of the Courtier* (1528), "the true and chief ornament of the mind is letters. . . . Let [the courtier] be versed in the poets. . . . Let him also be trained in the writing of verse and prose."

Three hundred years later, the situation of the poet had drastically changed. The undermining of the aristocracy and the system of patronage, the spread of scientific rationalism, the shift from a domestic art to a marketplace art, as well as evolving attitudes toward the aesthetic object, all worked to the poet's disadvantage. While a direct correlation between large cultural overhauls and specific changes in art is always a risky proposition, it must be said that the growing advocacy of systemization and classification did not favor the embellishments and conceits found in poetic language. As for the decline of patronage and its effect on the arts, Oliver Goldsmith, in 1759, had this to say: "When the link between patronage and learning was entire, then all who deserved fame were in a position of attaining it . . . but this link now seems entirely broken. . . . A jockey, or a laced player, supplies the place of the scholar, poet, or man of virtue."

The rise and fall of poetry's dominance in the life of the mind, both private and public, is the subject of Christopher Clausen's *The Place of Poetry,* and it arrives at an inhospitable and therefore especially opportune moment. At a time when our most influential critics are tightening the hermeneutic circle around the act of composition and the act of interpretation, often seeming to

limit the appreciation of poetry to critics, and only privileged ones
at that, it is both bracing and instructive to come across a study
that places poetry squarely back in the world. Clausen's argument
is disarmingly straightforward: Since the middle of the eighteenth
century, poets and critics have denied or gradually disregarded the
intellectual responsibilities of poetry, and this has "in all proba-
bility" accounted for the decline of the poetic audience. One reason for this abdication had been the ascendancy of science during
the past three hundred years. Increasingly threatened by the acad-
emies' embrace of science as the only true heuristic medium, men
of letters have resorted to making increasing claims for poetry.
This defense took two forms: (1) poetry, like science, conveyed
truths about the world; or (2) poetry, within its own scheme,
represented an integral and self-sufficient aesthetic, apart from the
world. The first proposition was further divided into what Clausen
refers to as the "hard argument"—the assertion that poetry is
nothing less than a prophetic vision of the universe—and the "soft
argument," which, in Matthew Arnold's famous words, upheld
poetry as "a criticism of life . . . capable of wonderfully helping us
to relate the results of modern science to our need for conduct, our
need for beauty." Eloquent though this plea is, it did not, in
Clausen's opinion, check the spreading notion that poetry was
essentially childish and irrelevant.

Nonetheless, a resurgence of public interest in poetry oc-
curred in the late nineteenth century with the publication, in 1861,
of Francis Palgrave's *Golden Treasury of the Best Songs and Lyrical
Poems in the English Language.* This anthology, which is still in
print in updated versions, succeeded in fixing in the public mind a
conception of poetry that dramatically simplified both its form and
function. Nonsatirical poetry dealt exclusively with love, death,
religion, war, external nature, and recollections of childhood. And
to be "poetical," a poem had to be short, unambiguous, and

lyrical—i.e., turning "on some single thought, feeling, or situation." With *Palgrave* in hand, Her Majesty's officers and civil
servants could bring to the farthest edges of the Empire proof of a
secure and pastoral England.

The outbreak of World War I shattered this conventional picture of England. Conventional attitudes about poetry, however,
remained largely intact among ordinary readers, despite the emergence of the modernist movement. In fact, Clausen contends that
one reason why the nonacademic audience for poetry is so small
today is the "enormous gap in taste" between the heirs of modernism (those who write and study poetry) and ordinary readers (who
hark back to *Palgrave*). The irony here is that in ridding itself of
formal characteristics and adopting free verse to portray the world
more realistically, in language approximating the vocabulary and
rhythms of ordinary discourse, poetry succeeded in losing what
little audience it had left.

Because we tend to think that the debate over the poem's
usefulness began in the nineteenth century, it is good to be reminded that in the intellectually charged atmosphere of the mid-
eighteenth and early-nineteenth centuries, the question of poetry's validity aroused strong feelings. Indeed, as soon as it was
suggested that poetry could not fully participate in the rationalistic and scientific order, poets responded by claiming that Nature
was, in fact, neither orderly nor schematic, but a mysterious, vital
force that only seers and poets could tap into. "God is a poet,
not a mathematician," asserted the German philosopher Johann
Herder. The growing division between the poet and the scientist,
between poet and serious man of affairs, would evolve into a see-
saw battle in which every writer, it seemed, felt obliged to air his
views. For Jeremy Bentham, poetry was about as valuable as push-
pin. Thomas Love Peacock likened the poet to "a semi-barbarian
in a civilized community." Shelley countered with his famous *De-*

fense, in 1821, defining poets as "hierophants of an unapprehended inspiration." Unimpressed, the young Macaulay, in his 1825 essay on Milton, speculated that, as "civilization advances, poetry almost necessarily declines . . . the vocabulary of an enlightened society is philosophical, that of a half-civilized people is poetical." Later in the century, Karl Marx found himself wondering whether the *Iliad* was compatible with the printing press; and Baudelaire, no fan himself of the moneyed classes, griped that no one would raise an eyebrow if a bourgeois ordered roast poet for dinner.

There were, of course, exceptions to the general rule that poets were stragglers on the road to progress. Victor Hugo in France, and Goethe in Germany, riding the crest of nationalistic feeling stirred up by the Napoleonic wars, were held up as great men, as well as great poets. In Victorian England, Browning and Tennyson basked in the public's esteem, and if, as Clausen believes, the cultural influence of poetry was past its peak by 1870, some volumes of poetry continued to earn large profits. Nevertheless, the fact that many households contained a copy of *In Memoriam* should not obscure the difference between the cult of the poet and the poet's intellectual clout.

In the aftermath of the Industrial Revolution, the emotional thrust of poetry seemed at odds with bourgeois culture's desire for order and respectability. Poets knew this and responded accordingly. If they could not lead, they also would not follow. Gautier, in his preface to *Mademoiselle de Maupin* (1834), gloried in the inutility of art; and a half century later, Rimbaud declared that "art is an imbecility"—soon followed by Valéry's assertion that "art is finally useless." Not all poets, however, were so quick to acquiesce to poetry's diminished role. Poetry had its place, but needed to earn it. "The time is not distant," Baudelaire wrote, in 1867, "when it will be understood that all literature which refuses to

march between science and philosophy is a homicidal and suicidal
literature." Stirring words, but would they be proven true? Neither
science nor philosophy would ever again be the province of poetry
in the sense that poets from Horace to Goethe understood them.

Although I have taken the liberty of augmenting Clausen's list
of poets, especially those outside England who had something to say about poetry's function, I haven't added anything new
to the historical overview. Nor do I think that Clausen himself
intended any great revelations to fall from the pages of this excel-
lent but all-too-brief study. What he has done, and it is no small
thing, is to remind us that art cannot exist in an intellectual vacuum
and that poets, as Lionel Trilling put it, must be seen as barome-
ters and also as part of the weather. The problem is that Clausen
shuttles so vigorously between points of view that we are left with a
polemical tract in which there is too much grist for the mill to grind
properly. By invoking the specter of cultural history, he finds himself, within his brief compass, either standing pat on certain judgments or hedging his bets on others. For example, he says that at
one time "the unity of the poem reflected the unity of the world,
something that the poetic imagination had found, not made." No
argument there—but what happened to shake this confidence?
What occurred between the time when Sir Thomas Browne felt
capable of describing reality as "that universal and public Manu-
script" and today when the depiction of reality—to use Clausen's
own words—"has come for many poets to mean the documentation of often meaningless details"? If this is asking too much, it is
Clausen himself who invites such speculations.

But it is a measure of Clausen's thoughtful survey—and I do
not mean to damn with faint praise—that he makes us realize that
the issues are more complicated than is his presentation of them.

How, for example, did nationalism and the belief in the individual affect the place of poetry? What were the attitudes and expectations of the emerging literate working class toward poetry? More important, were not all kinds of thinking during the eighteenth and nineteenth centuries subsumed under the idea of progress? Clausen gives short shrift to the idea that every discipline looked for its meaning in the scientific systematization of its parts and considered itself more or less bound to truth by its affinity to such classification. Thus, to a significant extent, attempts to defend poetry were in keeping with the intellectual temper of the times, which redefined everything in light of the scientific method.

One presupposition of Clausen's book is that "important poetry conveys significant ideas normally intended to apply to the world outside the poem." Thus fortified, Clausen argues that modernist poets, in spite of their determination to fashion autonomous works that are not beholden to the world, cannot avoid apprehending and articulating a world view. In fact, once we get past what modernist poets said about poetry and the technical flourishes of the poems themselves, their poems are "very much what one might have expected to find half a century after Arnold and Hopkins."

It was only *after* modernism—which ceased to be itself as soon as it became established—that poets struck out for more distant theoretical shores, where everything could be exploited for poetry's pleasure. Believing that the meaning of poetry lay in increasingly insurrectionary means of expression, poets removed themselves further and further from a general audience, retreating finally into a "demoralized solipsism." At the time, the choice seemed to be: either address the anxiety inherent in the latest threat to poetry's relevance or else retreat into a showy aestheticism that would, in its own way, be as obscure and difficult as the language of theorists and scientists. "Breaking the pentameter, that was the first heave," exulted Ezra Pound, and poets have been heaving ever since. Although it can be argued that the first modernists did reflect the dislocation of poetry from the world, fashioning poems whose shape and tonality took precedence over ideas, subsequent schools simply dismissed the tension, withdrawing to concentrate on elliptical and/or exclusively personal poetry. Soon there was nothing to stop poets from indulging in image-laden, freewheeling verse that delivered neurotic, charmless, though sometimes quotable, rants about life that only a critic or the poet's mother could love. In 1942, Eliot looked around and sighed: "A great deal of bad prose has been written under the name of free verse."

A quarter century later, another seminal poet, W. H. Auden, looked around and, seeing the wonders wrought by scientists and mathematicians, likened himself to "a shabby curate who strayed by mistake into a drawing room full of dukes." How was the poet to reflect the displacement and loss of certainties ushered in by analytic philosophy, relativity, and quantum mechanics? Could ordinary or even heightened language somehow demonstrate the priority of the invisible world of atoms over the visible world of objects? And this, of course, is where it gets complicated. If a poet writes as a man of his time writes, and his assumptions and expectations about the world are formed by the intellectual currents flowing around him, then the very disjunction (and perceived disparity) between humane letters and science must be reflected in his verse. Yet if poets were to accept this restriction, would they not be practicing an art that basically chewed on its own tail and had no resonance in the "real" world? Auden's rueful assessment that poetry makes nothing happen may be a rhetorical gambit, but it springs from a well-founded insecurity.

Fifty years ago, R. P. Blackmur had this to say about the state of the art:

There was at hand for Dante, and as a rule in the great ages of
poetry, a fundamental agreement or convention between the
poet and his audience about the validity of the view of life of
which the poet deepened the reality and spread the scope.
There is no such agreement today. We find poets either using
the small conventions of the individual life as if they were large
conventions, or attempting to resurrect some great convention
of the past, or, finally, attempting to discover the great convention that must lie, willy-nilly, in the life about them.

For Clausen, the situation remains much the same. The same
spool of film is being run repeatedly on numerous projectors.
Poets continue to invest the quotidian with transcendent values,
shaping a bright nimbus around life's trivia. Although there are
some serious-minded, technically inventive poets around today
(Clausen singles out John Hollander, Derek Walcott, A. D. Hope,
and Judith Wright), poetry itself does not demonstrate a significant
re-presentation of the world. Whether this is because poets feel no
responsibility to, or are unable to, view the world as a coherent,
ultimately comprehensible system, or because reality itself now
begins outside verbal language, are questions that Clausen wisely
lets pass.

Yet a demand for poetry exists. Poetry is even enjoying a
renaissance, if we are to believe James Atlas, writing in the *New
York Times Sunday Magazine* (1980). I doubt, however, that this is
the case. Nor do I think Clausen believes it to be. The reason that
poetry remains the road less traveled is best explained by Clausen
himself: "It is doubtful that at any time in the past many people
have read poetry entirely for esthetic pleasure. . . . Most people
have always expected poetry to illuminate some significant aspect
of life, in lines that stick in the mind." This is undeniably a reductive analysis of poetry's function and appeal, and Clausen is certain
to be chastised for what appears to be nostalgia for a more tradi-

tional prosody. He may even be accused of mistaking his own difficulties with contemporary poetry for some imagined failing in the poetry itself. But readers of poetry would do well to consider his objections: it is not the clothes that don't exist, but the emperor himself who is becoming invisible.

O
ne of the problems with defining poetry's cultural role, as indeed with that of every art form, is the lurking recognition that art is never entirely free of a certain elitism, even when it is enlisted in the service of mass social movements. Serious poetry— that is, poetry that does not shy from intellectual instruction— presumes an educated audience. The question of how many knowledgeable readers are required for serious poetry to flourish is academic—perhaps in both senses of the word. For Walt Whitman, the most angelically democratic of poets, in order "to have great poets, there must be great audiences too." It is pretty to think so, but Milton's more modest verdict of a "fit audience though few" is closer to the truth and perhaps all that poets can hope to expect.

All this is somewhat of a simplification—and yet that heuristic element that readers once expected from poetry is now largely absent. The world is not better understood for reading modern poems, though poetry itself may be better understood the more one reads in it. And if such poetry has beauty or interest, honesty also compels us to admit that not that much depends on a red wheelbarrow glazed with rain water, except the arrangement and sounds of those particular words. Nor is this the modern poet's fault. Not to put too fine a point on it, a poetry that seeks to interpret the modern world in all its difficulty and variety is, if successful, more physics than poetry. On the other hand, a poetry that retracts toward pure formalism or balloons into the solipsistic ranting of those who feel inclined to write "poems" is hardly what is wanted either. Ninety years ago, P. G. Wodehouse tendered the sly observation that "our children grow to adolescence with the feeling they can become poets instead of working," thus hitting the mark before there was even a mark to hit.

Has much changed? When a young poet I know was asked what she deemed essential in poetry, she replied that she expected poetry to present startling images in honest language that over-turned complacent and conventional attitudes. Poetry, she in-sisted, had to be true to the rawness of life; otherwise, it was "just silly." When asked what place beauty, music, and intellect had in poetry, she didn't hesitate: such things, she said, were archaic. She may be right. The times bring their own expectations. To my mind, contemporary verse—arriving from poets as diverse as Amy Clampitt and John Ashbery—has the look and feel of a concen-trated elliptical prose, a sort of elegant and tightly focused short-hand for making detailed observation. Such poems, as Thomas Mallon wittily observed, are nothing more than "prose that has been annoyed into verse." And far from much of it being bad prose, as Eliot suggested, a lot of it is actually pretty good prose. It may, in fact, be the age's perfect literary expression, and perhaps that's not such a terrible thing. Although each new generation of artists must assimilate and depict a world that has never before existed in quite the same way, not all generations are as fortunate as those that came of age during the late Renaissance, or at the turn of the nineteenth century, or during the first quarter of the twentieth century, when dramatic shifts in science, art, and perspective oc-curred. If the poetry of an age (or painting or sculpture or music or architecture) never achieves a luminous glow that extends into the future, so be it. A future will arrive soon enough in which great art shall again flourish—or it won't.

All one can say for certain is that the artist, if he is to impress his genius on a particular tradition, must provide a deeper under-standing of the relation between the personal and the historical, between new-found knowledge and age-old wisdom. In short, poets must teach us by whatever literary means they choose or invent what it means to live in any particular time. No matter the name or classification given to the poetic movement, the work is always more than just a matter of *techne* and talent: "Poetry is certainly something more than good sense," Coleridge wrote, "but it must be good sense . . . just as a palace is more than a house but it must be a house."

No doubt, there are poets at work today who construct their houses carefully and responsibly and who manifest a discerning intelligence in everything they write. The only thing is, they don't make us want to spend our lives in their houses; they don't persuade us that the world of their poems is the world we know, and that the words in their poems are the best possible words to explain how the world makes us feel. Of course, you may be of a different mind entirely and praise contemporary poets to the skies, but stop and think: Who among us can honestly say, as Eliot said of Yeats, "He was one of those few whose history is the history of their own time, who are part of the consciousness of an age which cannot be understood without them"?

[1982]

16

The Writing Life

————

Writers are different from other people. Not all writers—not those who write only for wages—but the poets, novelists, and essayists who believe they have no choice in the matter, who feel no less compelled to write than to think, and who therefore receive the continuing news of their existence as potential lines on a page. For them, what happens happens in order to be turned into verse or prose. And so literature itself may be understood as sheer ego channeled into print, undertaken with the perfect conviction that experience is concluded only upon being written down.

What an extraordinary assumption! What's wrong with living one's life without consecrating it to the written word? Why imagine that one's thoughts and feelings must be shared with others? Such intimacy, even when arriving in the guise of fiction, seems shameless, for despite the liberties novelists take with events, they are in the business of making private moments public. Like the spy as true believer, novelists subsume the fate and feelings of others to the greater good. Graham Greene, a writer who knew something about spying, felt there was "a splinter of ice in the heart of a writer"—a splinter, one might add, that could serve as an ice pick.

This lesson was forcibly brought home to some New York socialites when Truman Capote, an old friend, skewered them in his story "À la Cote Basque." Indiscretions that had until then been kept in the family were now bruited in the pages of a national magazine. Amazed and hurt, Capote's rich pals dropped him. Oddly enough, Capote seemed shocked in return. Apparently, he had thought he could get away with pillorying his patrician friends in public. Finally realizing that he had burned his bridges to their penthouses and estates, Capote pathetically complained, "But they know I'm a writer. I don't understand it."

Lack of comprehension, however, is usually on the side of non-writers, those hard-pressed to understand how a friend could betray them in print. Why should they understand? They aren't writers, the writing life is not life as they know it, and no explanation can justify the writer's behavior. It's an apt tag, "the writing life," the two words expressing a symbiotic relation while simultaneously blurring the distinction between them. Writing is a profession, we know, but it is also something more; otherwise doctors would talk of the "medical life" and lawyers of the "legal life." Curiously, the only other means of earning a living that is referred to as "a life" is prostitution. Prostitutes talk about what they do as being "in the life," and, like writers, theirs is a way of life that impedes living unself-consciously, denying them full participation in experience.

Both the writer and the prostitute detach themselves from certain moments in life in order to practice their trades; both detach themselves from experience in order to make others more aware of it. Perhaps prostitutes can make love honestly when not with a trick; writers, however, sooner or later treat all of life as a trick, something to turn to their advantage. All this may be an exaggeration, but what writer would deny that the psychology of the literary artist, insofar as it is different from other people's, consists in the cultivation of the self for the expressed purpose of communicating the self's progress through life?

Kierkegaard says somewhere that there are two ways to live: one can suffer or one can be a professor of another's suffering. By "professor," Kierkegaard means someone protected from terrible suffering by highly developed faculties of observation and contemplation. If only in this regard, Kierkegaard's professor resembles Nietzsche's "Artist," someone who lives at a remove from life's most deeply felt moments. Artists, writes Nietzsche, are not men of great passion, being far too busy interpreting themselves to have any shame about themselves. Nor can they feel shame before great passion, since they are always exploiting passion in their art. The compulsion to use life to beget art, Nietzsche tells us, smacks of vampirism, a draining of emotion that would ordinarily be spent in passion.

Sounds good, but are there indisputable truths about the artistic temperament? To what degree, if any, is the artist more self-conscious than the non-artist, and how do we go about measuring the difference? Is it fair to say that the artist or the professor of suffering is less in step with the ordinary rhythms of life than someone who does not reflect on those rhythms? And finally, we might ask whether the two temperaments are mutually exclusive. Nietzsche evidently believed so, professing that one either lives *or* that one lives as an artist—that is, one either suffers *or* one is a professor of others' suffering.

Of course, it is only writers and intellectuals who gnaw at these questions, wondering whether writing prevents them from knowing life in a way that other people know it. The anxiety comes with the territory. Someone always thinking about how to transform experience into art may be unable to appreciate the experience for what it really is—as if too much awareness of living must get in the way of living. Henry James, who believed that the writer should be someone on whom nothing is lost, also knew that this creed makes it impossible to lose oneself in experience. And this ambivalence about art overriding life explains much about James's own art and life. Yeats too felt the conflict: "The intellect of man is forced to choose / Perfection of the life, or of the work." Never totally at ease with the choice he made, Yeats would record his doubts in a poignant journal entry: "I might have lived instead." But like James, Yeats never really had a choice in the matter. He could no more have "lived instead" than not tied Ireland and Maud Gonne to poetry. Everything was linked to poetry, because in some sense everything was not enough *without* poetry.

So what is missing—what is missing that creates the need to write? Peace of mind is as good an answer as any, for what writer—or philosopher for that matter—begins work because he or she is at peace with the world? Novalis thought *philosophy* but another word for *homesickness,* the wish to feel everywhere at home; and down through the years more than one writer has mused that writing is an attempt to recapture the warmth and comfort of childhood (and home) or viewed it as a means to imagine a security never known at all. Possibly this nostalgia for a world either lost or never possessed underlies all serious literary work, since the very act of creation implies a certain lacking or failure in the world.

To speak of such matters evokes a philosophical preoccupation that may not, at first, seem pertinent to poetry and fiction. All the same, if existence were sufficient to make us satisfied with our knowledge of existence, we'd feel little desire to philosophize or to create. We would, in short, already be home. But the world is not, for those who make a fetish of consciousness, the repository of absolute answers. Something is, if not wrong, then beyond understanding; and, as philosophers like to tell us, consciousness itself keeps knowledge and truth a synapse apart.

Many writers, of course, live and work without excessive angst; for others, however, the insoluble question of why there is something rather than nothing claws and tears. Or perhaps the question just sits at the bottom of consciousness like a large metaphysical crab that makes everything seem heavier than it ought to be. It is a question, I believe, that helped drive Nietzsche to the conclusion (before madness set in) that all philosophy is at bottom "a secret raging against the preconditions of life." Or to put it in less charged terms: existence is a mystery, a goad to those who are fated to detect and deduce, an itch that leads to the scratching of a pen.

And if the pen knows anything at all, it knows that one day it must stop moving—that, too, is part of the mystery. Death waits, and we, each in our own way, go to meet it. This is not to suggest that death must constantly figure in literature but to acknowledge that the literature which matters is always about the triumph or failure of the human spirit, a struggle that would be meaningless if life itself were not, in the end, terminal. So while mortality may not define the scope of literature, it does suggest the subtext of creativity, the point where the desire to create and the end of all creation meet.

Just as consciousness precludes the positing of intellectual absolutes, it also underlines the one truth none of us may escape. Death shadows us, and in a sense death creates us, shaping how we think and act. A being whose existence is eternal would probably not inquire too deeply into its meaning or demand the reassurances that mortals clamor for. Nor perhaps would beauty loom large in paradise if, as Wallace Stevens believed, death is the mother of beauty. What need for beauty in life everlasting? Would anyone debate the point that we find beauty in life because life itself is so brief, that we create art because art is not part of creation, and that we philosophize because we can never be sure that knowledge is synonymous with truth?

Of course, not even philosophers and board-certified melancholics dwell constantly on their own deaths. No one lives as if he or she were about to keel over. Death shadows us but does not darken the ground on which we walk, and even the gloomiest thinker may be interrupted by life's more trivial crises. Nowhere is this more nicely sketched than in Balzac's *La Peau de chagrin* at the point when the young hero pauses to reflect on all the dead civilizations that have come and gone. He contemplates the pitifully brief time we have on this earth and wonders whether our triumphs, loves, failures, and hatreds really amount to anything, if we are only to become an undetectable speck in the future. Clearly, it is all meaningless, all for nothing—until, that is (here Balzac jumps in), a valet enters the room to announce: "*Madame la comtesse* says that she is expecting you." Suddenly things are definitely looking up. Suddenly life is filled with promise. Yes, it's the rare philosopher whose existential suffering cannot be softened by a pair of soft arms.

But what sort of suffering is this? Surely not the kind requisite to the production of profound works of art or philosophy. The contemplative spirit, if it intends to represent the human condition, must have its nose in the muck of human experience, inhaling love, pain, failure, success, joy, and heartache, without which the act of thinking becomes an abstract exercise in self-consciousness. Indeed, in extreme cases, when the body must scrabble to exist, metaphysics is a luxury beyond the reach of even the most self-conscious. In other words, there comes a point when neither the artist nor the philosopher, however much he may desire or feel it necessary, can avoid the passion and suffering that an imperfect world doles out.

Consider the case of Primo Levi, a writer whose tortured self-consciousness embraced both passion and suffering. As a young man, Levi had spent more than a year in Auschwitz, and though he became a writer, he never became a professor of suffering; though an artist, he still felt great shame in living. Anyone who has read Levi's *The Drowned and the Saved* cannot help having been struck by the confession of shame he felt while in the camps. It was shame that had nothing to do with the fact that he survived while millions died but with what he saw and endured. In a terrible way, it makes sense. The horror, the horrible enormity of the event, precludes the idea of innocence. Why should someone suffer so much, have so much cruelty inflicted on mind and body, if one is truly innocent? Life had shamed Levi, and there was nothing he could do, he admitted, to rid himself of this shame.

He wrote books, both fiction and non-fiction, but did they comprehend or communicate what happened? If writing was a way of bearing witness and of revealing what man is capable of, it was for Levi also a way of dealing with memory, of sustaining life against the wish to erase the knowledge stored in memory. But eventually this knowledge overwhelmed him. More than forty years after he left the *lagers,* Auschwitz finally released him. Levi committed suicide—not because he was an artist or a professor of suffering, but because there came a moment when art could no longer save him, when the shame of experience finally became more powerful than the wish to create from that experience. It was then that Primo Levi chose to become nothing rather than something.

Whatever the degree of self-consciousness involved in the writing life, total detachment is not possible; if it were, people would never think to write, and writers never think to take their own lives. "A literary artist, besides being in a sense immune from experience," observed Desmond MacCarthy, "must also be at the mercy of it, so that he cannot tell afterwards whether he has owed more to the naive impulses which drove him to meet life, or to the aloofness which softly and inevitably disentangled him again." This seems a fairer statement than Nietzsche's strictures regarding the artist's susceptibility to great passion. The writer, in fact, may both feel and exploit passion, and whether he feels it any less intensely than others is not for us to say.

The more commonly held opinion, of course, is that artists feel more deeply than non-artists, being more sensitive to the vicissitudes of life. Who knows? It is just as likely that literary artists have no special dispensation when it comes to feeling. What separates them from non-artists is not a special capacity for joy or suffering but the need to transform their emotional life into art and the realization that they have precious little choice in the matter. One does not ask to be a poet or novelist (only poseurs aspire to the title); one writes because there's no help for it, because one doesn't really have a choice in the matter.

If there is a defining characteristic of those who are compelled to bend the sounds and nuances of words to their will, it might be the notion that writing, more than being just a force in one's life, is a means of making sense of that life. To write about life and to live are reciprocal modes of being. The person who writes and the person who lives complement each other, each feeds off the other, each strives for the knowledge that may help both to understand themselves.

In his letters, John Keats articulates the consciousness of a man striving to know himself. Thinking about the soul, not in the strictly Christian sense but as a means for individual fulfillment, he writes to his brother George that the soul is an *"Intelligence destined to possess the sense of Identity."* But identity is not so easy to acquire. Being a poet, he thinks himself "the most unpoetical of any thing in existence; because he has no Identity": he too readily fills other bodies and enters other minds; he is too "capable of being in uncertainties." Now, while this gives him material to write about, it also causes him great distress. "I live under an everlasting restraint," he confides, "never relieved except when I am composing—So I will write away."

Few writers deserve our gratitude more than Keats for writing away. The irony, of course, is that we profit by his distress, just as we benefit from the discomfort that compels all great writers to write. That "everlasting restraint" is the burden of self-consciousness, which stimulates composition in order to define further its own nature. Keats's relief when writing is not the result of conquering his inhibitions; it is based in the activity of realizing the self. When composing, he composes himself; composing, he lets his Intelligence create its Identity.

That is perhaps the closest we may come to understanding the writing life, a life intent on acquiring an identity as both artist and individual. What does a poem or novel say except this is what happened, this is what I learned, and this is, insofar as I am able to say, who I am? Every literary work thus becomes the ghost of someone who once passed this way. "Whoever touches this [book]," Walt Whitman promised, "touches a man." These are the ghosts that, one hopes, will continue to haunt us. For it is comforting to know that somewhere, at some time, a person felt the need to speak, who looked at a sheet of paper and stained the uninviting whiteness of eternity with the small, irregular symbols that, whatever their shape and however their arrangement, always say: Know Me.

[1998]

Credits

Chapter 1. *Harper's,* March 1996.

Chapter 2. *American Scholar,* Spring 1998.

Chapter 3. Published as: "On Writing—Let There Be Less," Front Page, *New York Times Book Review,* March 26, 1989.

Chapter 4. *American Scholar,* Spring 1999.

Chapter 5. *Harper's,* February 2001.

Chapter 6. *American Scholar,* Autumn 2001.

Chapters 7–11. Mss.

Chapter 12. Review of Geoffrey H. Hartman's *Minor Prophecies: The Literary Essay in the Culture Wars. American Scholar.* Autumn 1992.

Chapter 13. Front Page, *New York Times Book Review,* June 9, 1985.

Chapter 14. Expanded review of James Engell's *The Creative Imagination: Enlightenment to Romanticism. American Scholar.* Spring 1984.

Chapter 15. Expanded review of Christopher Clausen's *The Place of Poetry: Two Centuries of an Art in Crisis. American Scholar.* Autumn 1982.

Chapter 16. *American Scholar,* Spring 1997.